New Vanguard • 126

British Battlecruisers 1914–18

Lawrence Burr • Illustrated by Tony Bryan

First published in Great Britain in 2006 by Osprey Publishing,
Midland House, West Way, Botley, Oxford OX2 0PH, UK
44-02 23rd St, Suite 219, Long Island City, NY 11101, USA
E-mail: info@ospreypublishing.com

A CIP catalogue record for this book is available from the British Library

ISBN: 978 1 84603 008 6

Page layout by Melisa Orrom Swan
Index by Alan Thatcher
Originated by PPS Grasmere Ltd., Leeds, UK
Printed in China through World Print Ltd.
Typeset in Helvetica Neue and ITC New Baskerville
10 11 12 13 14   14 13 12 11 10 9 8 7 6 5

FOR A CATALOGUE OF ALL BOOKS PUBLISHED BY OSPREY
MILITARY AND AVIATION PLEASE CONTACT:

Osprey Direct, c/o Random House Distribution Center,
400 Hahn Road, Westminster, MD 21157
Email: uscustomerservice@ospreypublishing.com

Osprey Direct, The Book Service Ltd, Distribution Centre,
Colchester Road, Frating Green, Colchester, Essex, CO7 7DW
Email: customerservice@ospreypublishing.com

www.ospreypublishing.com

Author's acknowledgements

The author wishes to acknowledge the help and assistance provided by:
Captain Christopher Page RN (Rtd), Jenny Wraight and Iain MacKenzie of
the Naval Historical Branch for suggesting original documents to read, and
showing great patience in helping the author appreciate the significance of the
contents from a naval perspective. Mr. Suddaby of the Imperial War Museum
for introducing me to the Jutland files and Captain Grant's unpublished
memoirs. Dr Andrew Gordon, Dr Nicholas Lambert and Professor Jon Sumida
for their time in discussing with me the intricacies of naval culture and tactics,
the myriad issues and events surrounding the development of fire control and
the development of naval strategy, as well as suggesting further reading. I am
particularly indebted to Professor Sumida for sharing with me his research
identifying the fire-control systems installed in each battlecruiser, and
Dr Lambert for sharing with me his research. Evelyn Cherpak, Curator, US
Naval War College, for introducing me to the Jutland files of the Naval Historical
Collection. My good friend Innes McCartney, for describing what he saw when
diving on the battlecruiser wrecks, and sharing with me all his video footage
taken on the shipwrecks. Finally, my wonderful wife, Judi, for her support and
unfailing good humour as naval charts and ship plans took over the house.

Editor's note

Imperial War Museum Collections

Many of the photos in this book come from the Imperial War Museum's
huge collections, which cover all aspects of conflict involving Britain and the
Commonwealth since the start of the twentieth century. These rich resources
are available online to search, browse and buy at www.iwmcollections.org.uk.
In addition to Collections Online, you can visit the Visitor Rooms where you can
explore over 8 million photographs, thousands of hours of moving images, the
largest sound archive of its kind in the world, thousands of diaries and letters
written by people in wartime, and a huge reference library. To make an
appointment, call (020) 7416 5320, or e-mail mail@iwm.org.uk.
Imperial War Museum www.iwm.org.uk

BRITISH BATTLECRUISERS 1914–18

INTRODUCTION

British battlecruisers are described as a 'flawed design based upon an ill-thought through strategic concept' advanced by Admiral Fisher, First Sea Lord, 1904–10. These comments were primarily made based upon three British battlecruisers blowing up, with heavy loss of life, during the battle of Jutland on 31 May 1916. Additionally, the reports by Admirals Jellicoe and Beatty, that the loss of *Indefatigable*, *Queen Mary* and *Invincible* was due to the lack of armour protection, established this point at the forefront of any analysis of British battlecruisers.

Recent analysis by leading naval historians, based upon exhaustive research of Admiralty files, and surveys of the wrecks of the sunken ships, strongly challenges this critical view of British battlecruisers. Far from being a 'wrong turn in warship design', they embodied futuristic concepts on the global projection of sea-power. It was neither the design nor Admiral Fisher's strategic concept for battlecruisers that was flawed, but the operation of this new weapons system.

British battlecruisers were a highly successful class of warship. The introduction of the battlecruiser represented more than a revolution in shipbuilding. Battlecruisers married naval technological developments with communication and intelligence-gathering breakthroughs, wedded together in a Global War Room at the Admiralty in London. This allowed, for the first time, rapid strategic and tactical deployment of scarce naval resources by the Admiralty for the defence of trade and sea communications with the Empire and for command of the sea.

HMS *Invincible*, newly commissioned, 1909. The tall topmasts for the aerials of the long-range wireless equipment are clearly visible. Note the two 4-in. guns on top of A turret, and the spotting top on the foremast. (Imperial War Museum (IWM))

ADMIRAL FISHER AND THE TRANSFORMATION OF THE NAVY

When Admiral Fisher became First Sea Lord in October 1904, he was faced with a range of major issues that were threatening Britain's command of the seas. These included strategic threats from an alliance between Russia and France, with a burgeoning French Navy whose development of the 'belted cruiser' (the first cruiser with armoured sides) was designed to attack Britain's food supplies and trade routes, thus potentially changing the nature of naval warfare from fleet vs. fleet combat at close range. In response to the alliance, Britain

passed the Naval Defence Act 1889, introducing a 'Two Power Standard' dictating that the Royal Navy had to develop a fleet equal to the combined fleet of the next two largest naval powers. Additionally, the advances in naval technology proved a double-edged sword for the Royal Navy. Naval technology had developed at a rapid rate since the launch of the French warship *La Gloire* in 1860, the first ocean-going ironclad. Later the same year the Admiralty launched the first iron-hulled frigate, *Warrior*. The year 1862 saw the revolving gun turret; 1866, the trial of the first torpedo; 1868, the submerged torpedo tube; 1870, hydraulic power; 1874, electric power; 1876, armour plate; 1879, breech-loading guns; 1881, electric-range transmitter; 1883, rapid-fire guns; 1884, turbine engines; 1885, armour-piercing shells; 1886, high-pressure boilers; 1888, nitroglycerine/cellulose based propellants and high explosives; 1890, director firing and stereoscopic rangefinders; 1891, telescopic gun sight and automatic plot for fire control; 1894, nickel-steel armour plate; 1895, watertight compartments; 1890, the Holland submarine. These new technologies,the tactics for using and countering them, and their impact on strategy, had to be factored into ship construction. They also meant that the earlier warship designs were rapidly becoming obsolete and expensive to maintain. The operating cost of the Royal Navy's fleet, the ongoing construction costs for new ships, plus the recruitment and training of new crews, represented a major drain on the government's budget. This coincided with a time of national fiscal deterioration, financial restraint and increasing political needs for social reform. Without radical change to lower the cost of the Royal Navy, Britain's command of the sea was at risk from budgetary cuts.

Fisher inherited a technologically strong navy with a cable communications network and developing wireless capability that ensured the Admiralty in London could communicate globally. The communications network was also supported by naval intelligence. In 1901 the Naval Intelligence Department established a new section to identify the flow and routes of maritime trade to and from Britain, thus allowing the Admiralty to see 'at a glance where British merchant vessels are most likely to be found in the greatest numbers at different times of the year'. The Admiralty developed this further by using local consuls, shipping agents and secret agents, who supplied them with details of ship positions and movements over the cable network. Additionally, the Admiralty accessed the shipping intelligence of Lloyds of London. This intelligence network and charting identified both merchant ships and foreign warships and became the basis of the 'War Room' at the Admiralty in 1906.

Fisher's transformation
Fisher's response to these issues was to transform the Navy radically. The rapidly developing Admiralty infrastructure of global cable and wireless

Indomitable and *Inflexible* showing the large amounts of smoke created at high speed, blotting out visibility. Seen after Jutland, the gun director and training scale on A turret are clearly visible. (IWM)

HMS _Indomitable_ showing A and P gun turrets. Six 12-in. guns could fire forward, maximizing end-on-fire when chasing the enemy. (IWM)

communication networks, supported by intelligence gathering, enabled the Admiralty to change from its pre-technology role of overseeing the design and commissioning of warships and deciding the force level for each station to exerting operational control globally. This new strategic global infrastructure supported the development of a two-pronged naval strategy: sea-denial and rapid deployment.

Sea-denial reflected the geography of the narrow seas around Britain, and employed torpedoes, submarines and fast destroyers supported by pre-dreadnought battleships. This force structure protected Britain from invasion by posing an overwhelming torpedo threat to an invasion fleet. This strategy was named 'Flotilla Defence', and was intended to replace standing fleets of battleships which Fisher saw as being increasingly vulnerable to the torpedo.

Rapid deployment was based upon a new weapon system: the wireless-equipped fast and long-range battlecruiser carrying battleship armaments, operating in 'flying squadrons' with light cruisers, and able to intercept, run down, out-manoeuvre and out-gun any warship afloat. Admiralty-controlled 'flying squadrons' negated the need for large, expensive and ageing squadrons based on overseas naval stations. A key factor underpinning the rapid deployment strategy was the technological breakthroughs in fire control governing the accuracy of main armament gunfire. These developments promised accuracy at greater ranges whilst both firing and target ships made changes in course.

This two-pronged strategy enabled Fisher aggressively to reshape and reduce the financial cost of the Navy by recalling and scrapping 154 ships in 1905, and utilizing the manpower released to crew the new force of submarines, destroyers and battlecruisers. The new fast battlecruiser was the visible manifestation of the convergence of naval and communications technology with intelligence and war planning. This was no 'ill-thought through strategy' nor was the fast battlecruiser simply an evolution from previous armoured cruisers. It was a new naval concept which, in modern parlance, we call 'Network-Centric Warfare'.

COMMITTEE ON DESIGNS, 1904

Fisher appointed the Committee on Designs on 22 December 1904, to consider the design features of future battleships and armoured cruisers, later to be called battlecruisers. The Admiralty had already decided that these new ships would have uniform big-gun armament. This decision reflected developments in gunnery and the impact of the torpedo on the tactics of warships.

Advances in gunnery recognized that establishing gunnery supremacy (being able to hit at ranges beyond which the enemy could reply) at the outset of battle dictated the battle's outcome. As Fisher put it, 'Hit first, hit hard and keep on hitting.' In addition, the arming of ships with mixed-calibre guns made 'spotting' the fall of shot difficult and prevented accurate aim and range corrections. Salvo fire by uniform armament, aided by a 'control' officer located in a 'spotting top' on the foremast solved this problem. In addition, electrical communications between the various components of fire control and the gun turrets made salvo fire possible. Improvements in the application of hydraulic power made the loading and accurate training of 12-in. guns faster.

The Whitehead torpedo, first trialled in 1866, represented a major threat to large warships. The introduction of the gyroscope to the torpedo's guidance mechanism in 1898 significantly improved the torpedo's accuracy. The range and speed of the torpedo steadily increased and matched the range at which large guns could be accurately fired. This made the torpedo a major threat to the 'line of battle', consisting of warships sailing parallel to each other firing broadsides. Ship speed and long-range accurate gunnery were the only answers if warships were to keep out of the range of torpedoes and still fire at the enemy.

The main instructions given to the committee were:
'For the battleship:
Speed was to be 21 knots.
Armament was to be 12-in. guns, as numerous as consistent with the above speed, and anti-torpedo boat guns only.
Armour was to be adequate.
The ship was to be able to use existing docks at Portsmouth, Devonport, Malta and Gibraltar.
For the armoured cruiser:
Speed was to be 25 knots.
Armament was to be 12-in. guns, as numerous as consistent with the above speed, and anti-torpedo boat guns only.
Armour protection was to be on a similar scale as the *Minotaur* class.
Docking requirements were to be carefully observed.'

The committee debated the advantages of broadside fire vs. end-on-fire for the layout for the 12-in. gun turrets. The latter needed to be maximized when the ship was chasing a fleeing enemy. The blast effect of superfiring guns would enter through the open sighting hoods and gun ports on the lower turret and injure the gun crew. Therefore final designs had a single turret on the forecastle deck with two beam wing turrets situated amidships to maximize end-on-fire.

The other major design feature discussed was turbines. Only three destroyers had been fitted with turbines when the committee met, but transatlantic passenger liners fitted with turbines were setting speed records with regular scheduled Atlantic crossings. The committee decided to order turbines, which saved approximately 1,000 tons in weight compared with the reciprocating engines then commonly used to power all large warships.

A critical factor underpinning decisions regarding armour protection was that future actions would be fought at ranges of 9 to 10,000 yards (roughly 8 to 9,000m) where the trajectory of large-calibre shells would be flat. Additionally, the armour for the armoured cruiser would be more than sufficient against the medium-calibre shells of opposing armoured cruisers. Fisher's thinking on the importance of speed and a uniform one-calibre large gun armament was confirmed by the results of the battle of Tsushima in May 1905.

HMS *Indefatigable*, **the slip-of-the-tongue battlecruiser. Her increased length over** *Invincible* **allowed P and Q turrets to fire across beam for broadside fire. The tall topmasts are clearly shown. (IWM)**

The battleship *Dreadnought* was laid down on 2 October 1905, launched on 10 February 1906, and completed on 11 December 1906. The all-big-gun, turbine-driven *Dreadnought* gave her name to all battleships that followed her.

Whilst Fisher had achieved his aim for a battleship that was faster and better armed than any other battleship, he believed that the battleship itself was an obsolete concept vulnerable to the submarine and torpedo-boat, which were rapidly developing into potent weapons systems. Fisher saw the fast, heavily armed armoured cruiser, employed in 'flying squadrons' directed from the Admiralty, as the means by which the Royal Navy would maintain its command of the sea. The new armoured cruisers were to replace battleships as the Navy's major warship. Accordingly, three fast armoured cruisers were ordered, to the design criteria established by the committee, and included in the 1905 estimates with the *Dreadnought*. These ships became the *Invincible, Indomitable* and *Inflexible.*

COMPARISON OF *INVINCIBLE* WITH OTHER MAJOR SHIPS

Name	Length	Displacement	Armour Protection	Main Armament	Speed
Invincible	530ft (162m)	17,250 tons	Belt 6in. (15cm) Deck 1in. (2.5cm)	8 x 12-in.	25kt(+)
Dreadnought	490ft (150m)	17,900 tons	Belt 11in. (28cm) Deck 0.75in. (2cm)	10 x 12-in.	21kt
*Lord Nelson**	410ft (125m)	16,500 tons	Belt 12in. (30.5cm) Deck 1.75in. (4.5cm)	4 x 12-in.	18kt
Minotaur#	490ft (150m)	14,600 tons	Belt 6in. (15cm) Deck 2in. (5cm)	4 x 9.2-in.	23kt(-)

Note: * = pre-dreadnought battleship. # = pre-dreadnought armoured cruiser.

The additional length was necessary for the boilers and turbines to give the ship a significant margin of speed. In commission, all the *Invincible*-class ships exceeded their 25-knot stated speed. Fisher is quoted as saying 'speed equals protection'. As important, speed equalled rapid global deployment. The *Invincible* class represented, in today's terminology, the first global rapid-response naval taskforce.

BRITISH BATTLECRUISERS

The first nomenclature for the new ships was 'fast armoured cruiser'. However, as the difference between the *Invincible* class and that of prior armoured cruisers was so significant, in November 1911 the Admiralty introduced the term battlecruiser.

There were five classes of battlecruisers that served with the Royal Navy during the 1914–18 war. These were:

Invincible class, comprising three ships.

Indefatigable class, comprising three ships.

Lion class, comprising three ships.

Renown class, comprising two ships.

Courageous class, comprising two ships.

In addition, there were two one-off battlecruisers, *Tiger* and *Furious.*

The *Invincible* class

The *Invincible* class comprised *Invincible*, *Indomitable* and *Inflexible*. When these ships were commissioned 1908–09, they represented a massive leap forward in ship design. Capable of sailing at over 25 knots for days, they were 40ft (12m) longer and 4 knots faster than the *Dreadnought*. In addition, they outclassed all pre-dreadnought battleships and armoured cruisers, which could only steam at full speed for an hour or so. A key feature of these new ships was their very tall topmasts, needed to support the aerials for their long-range wireless sets.

With their massive ram bows, flat-sided funnels and powerful superstructure over their 12-in. gun turrets, the new battlecruisers projected an impressive and incomparable sense of aggressive naval power that characterized the Royal Navy.

The *Indefatigable* class

The *Indefatigable* class comprised *Indefatigable*, *New Zealand* and HMAS *Australia*. *New Zealand* and *Australia* were paid for by their respective governments, with *New Zealand* given as a gift to the Royal Navy. *Australia* became the flagship of the Royal Australian Navy, and in early 1915 was assigned to operate with the Grand Fleet. The design for the *Indefatigable* class has been heavily criticized for being simply an enlarged *Invincible*.

The naval budget for 1908 prepared in 1907–08 was overshadowed by a new Liberal government focused on social reform and welfare programmes. Additionally, the impact of the destruction of the Russian Fleet at Tsushima on the 'Two Power Standard' showed that Britain now enjoyed an unassailable lead of pre-dreadnought battleships.

The consequence was a significantly reduced construction budget proposing one dreadnought battleship and one armoured cruiser to be laid down in 1909. However, during a parliamentary debate on the Navy in March 1908, the Chancellor of the Exchequer, Asquith, made a slip of the tongue in his speech by mistakenly describing the armoured cruiser as a 'battlecruiser'. Asquith became Prime Minister one month later in April 1908 and Fisher saw the opportunity to upgrade the 'proposed' armoured cruiser to an 'approved' battlecruiser. This unique political situation, of not

HMS *Lion*, the 'splendid cat', in 1912. The first battlecruiser with superfiring gun turrets. The midships Q turret between the second and third funnels is also visible. The first battlecruiser to be larger than a comparable battleship. (IWM)

embarrassing a new prime minister, did not allow sufficient time for a new considered battlecruiser design to be formulated. Fisher had the *Invincible* design amended by lengthening the ship to allow for a better layout of the mid-ship gun turrets.

The *Lion* class

The *Lion* class, referred to as the 'splendid cats', comprised *Lion, Princess Royal* and *Queen Mary*. The ships reflected a significant development over both the *Invincible* and *Indefatigable* classes and comparable dreadnoughts of the *Orion* class. The development was a direct result of a major change in the strategic environment affecting Britain. Previously, Britain had structured its naval strategy on the basis of France and Russia being its main potential naval adversaries. By mid-1908, the implications of Germany's naval laws and dreadnought building programme had been identified as a serious threat to Britain. The Admiralty estimated that by 1912 Germany would have reached parity with Britain in the number of dreadnoughts built. This estimate was based upon the significantly reduced British construction budget approved in early 1908 by Parliament.

In Britain, a public campaign, 'We want eight and we won't wait', resulted in Parliament approving a marked increase in naval construction, including *Lion* and *Princess Royal*. Fisher wanted all eight approved ships to be built as battlecruisers. However, he was unable to convince the Board of Admiralty to support him. Germany was building dreadnoughts and therefore other members of the board believed Britain had to build them as well. Total reliance on a 'flotilla defence' of submarines and destroyers was too radical a strategy for them. In addition to the details of Germany's dreadnought building programme, the Admiralty also received design details of German battlecruisers. These revealed the thicker level of armour protection built into the ships.

The rapid change in the political attitude to naval shipbuilding can be seen from the following table whereby the *Lion* and *Princess Royal* were laid down before the two Dominion-funded ships, *New Zealand* and *Australia*, of the *Indefatigable* class. The significant increase in the cost of the new *Lion*-class battlecruisers was more than the Dominion governments could afford.

Name	Laid down	Launched	Commissioned
Indefatigable	February 1909	October 1909	February 1911
Lion	November 1909	August 1910	May 1912
Princess Royal	May 1910	April 1911	November 1912
New Zealand	June 1910	July 1911	November 1912
Australia	June 1910	October 1911	June 1913
Queen Mary	March 1911	March 1912	September 1913

With the intelligence on German naval construction, together with the removal of financial constraints on new ship construction costs, a radical development of battlecruiser design was completed. The *Lion* class was 105ft (32m) longer than the *Indefatigable* class, displaced 7,550 more tons, had thicker armour and carried the new and far more powerful 13.5-in. gun that shot a 1,250lb (570kg) shell, versus the 850lb (385kg) shell of the 12-in. gun. Finally, the *Lion* class was at least 3 knots faster, but its radius of action was lower.

As important, the *Lion* class displaced 3,850 tons more than the *Orion*-class battleship, which carried ten 13.5-in. guns. This was the first instance of a battlecruiser being larger than a comparable dreadnought. The increased size reflected the weight, size and number of boilers – 42 in the *Lion* versus 18 in the *Orion* – to generate the power for the high speed of the *Lion* class.

A changing Board of Admiralty

Fisher retired in January 1910, after overseeing the ordering of the *Lion*-class battlecruisers. Admiral Sir Arthur Wilson was appointed the new First Sea Lord. Wilson had been one of the Navy's eminent fleet commanders and fleet tacticians. The naval race with Germany being in full flight, Wilson concentrated upon establishing a 'Grand Fleet of Battle' to meet and defeat any German threat that might arise in the North Sea.

During the years 1910–11, Wilson took three decisions that were to have a critical impact on the operation of battlecruisers. First, the trials and development of the Argo plotter for fire control was seriously delayed and subsequently cancelled in favour of the inferior Dreyer table in 1912. Likewise, Wilson delayed the development of Captain Percy Scott's director system. In November 1911, Wilson countermanded a request for the design of a new armour-piercing shell. Gunnery trials in 1909–10 revealed that existing armour-piercing shells failed to pierce armour plate when they hit at an oblique angle, as occurred in long-range gunnery. This decision reflected the adoption of a policy that the Navy would use high-explosive shells at long range to disable the enemy's fire-control and command structures and then switch to armour-piercing shells at ranges of 10,000 yards (9,150m) or less.

In response to a public and parliamentary campaign for the Admiralty to adopt a Naval War Staff, as well as a war scare with the Agadir crisis in July 1911, the government appointed Winston Churchill as First Lord of the Admiralty in October 1911. In turn, Churchill appointed Admiral Bridgeman as First Sea Lord, replacing Wilson. Churchill took advice from the retired Admiral Fisher on a broad range of issues and became convinced of the necessity for battlecruisers to have high speed.

HMS *Tiger*

Tiger was a single ship and not a class of ships and the final considerations of her design felt the involvement of Winston Churchill, who requested additional ship horsepower for higher speed. She was an enlarged *Lion*

HMS *Tiger* in 1914. The grouping of her three funnels improved the arc of fire of the midships Q turret. *Tiger* was built with a gun director on the tripod foremast. Note the absence of torpedo nets and booms. (IWM)

class by 3,500 tons, with a better main gun turret layout. The secondary armament was increased from the 4-in. of the *Lion* class to 6-in. to counter the larger German torpedo boats that were expected to accompany the German Fleet to sea. *Tiger* was the first battlecruiser to be constructed with a director system as part of the original design, and the last battlecruiser to be built before the outbreak of the 1914–18 war with Germany.

The *Renown* class

Two ships composed the *Renown* class, *Renown* and *Repulse*, both laid down in January 1915. These were the first battlecruisers to be built after a three-year pause. During this period, 1912–15, ten dreadnoughts had been ordered, making up the *Queen Elizabeth* class and the *Royal Sovereign* class. At the outbreak of the war, construction of the dreadnoughts of the 1914 programme was delayed in order for the ships already being built to be completed during the war. Admiral Fisher returned to the Admiralty as First Sea Lord one day before the defeat at the battle of Coronel occurred. Success at the battles of the Falklands and the Heligoland Bight and the disappointment of the December 1914 operation, reinforced Fisher's belief in the importance of speed, especially in bad weather, and he received government approval to convert two of the planned dreadnoughts to fast battlecruisers.

Fisher saw the *Renown* class as a fast wing of the battlecruiser fleet, in their role of reconnaissance in force to locate the German Fleet. Fisher requested that the *Renown* class carry 25 mines, presumably to be sown as they retired from their reconnaissance if pursued by the enemy. However, this requirement was dropped after Fisher resigned from the Admiralty in May 1915.

The *Courageous* class

The *Courageous* class comprised two ships, *Courageous* and *Glorious*. These ships are best described as light battlecruisers. Their wartime origins reflect Fisher taking advantage of a poorly worded cabinet approval, similar to the slip-of-the-tongue origins of *Indefatigable*. Cabinet approval for ship construction in 1915 specified nothing larger than light cruisers. However, the size of light cruiser was not detailed and this gave Fisher the opportunity to build two large light cruisers with limited battlecruiser armament at 18,600 tons displacement.

The *Courageous*-class ships carry a myth that they were designed specifically for the Baltic expedition. This expedition was to land a million Russian soldiers on the Pomeranian coast 80 miles from Berlin under

HMS *Repulse* with the Forth Bridge in the background. Two stern triple 4-in. gun mountings and shields are clearly seen over X turret. *Repulse* was the first oil-powered and 15-in. gunned battlecruiser. (IWM)

cover of the Royal Navy. However, their design origins simply reflect the effects of heavy weather in the North Sea on light cruisers, coupled with a strategic assessment that German naval raids on Britain would most likely occur during the dark and bad weather of the winter months. The relatively shallow waters of the North Sea throw up steep waves in bad weather, and this reduced the speed of light cruisers to 15 knots or less. Dreadnoughts and battlecruisers were able to steam at a higher speed in the same weather. This meant that the scouting screen of light cruisers had to be curtailed or abandoned as they could not keep up with the fleet. Additionally, light cruisers would not be able to use their speed to escape if they met German dreadnoughts and battlecruisers in heavy weather. *Courageous* and *Glorious*, with their heavier displacement, were designed to punch through their opposite light cruiser screen and locate the German Fleet in any weather. Their relatively shallow draught gave them additional speed and the ability to pursue enemy ships into the shallow waters of the Heligoland Bight. *Courageous* and *Glorious* were as fast as German torpedo boats in any weather state other than calm seas.

HMS *Furious*

Furious was another single ship and not a class. She was originally designed as a sister ship to *Courageous* and *Glorious*, but was modified to carry two 18-in. guns in single gun turrets, one forward and one aft. *Furious* was originally a 'special service' ship to provide bombardment support off the Flanders coast. The displacement and beam were increased and the draught decreased to enable her to close the shallow coast. During construction the design for *Furious* was further modified, eliminating the forward 18-in. gun turret and replacing it with a 160ft (49m) flying-off deck for aircraft.

Furious was as revolutionary as *Invincible*. Fisher saw the battlecruiser as replacing the battleship because of its global reach, ability to outrun and outrange its enemy, and carrying and delivering the maximum weight of armament for its size. In *Furious*, the battlecruiser as a gunned ship started the transformation to carrying a new main armament

HMS *Furious* nearing completion in 1917. The sloping flying-off deck and the aft single 18-in. gun turret can be seen clearly. A hybrid battlecruiser/aircraft carrier. (IWM)

system, the bomb- and torpedo-armed aircraft. Aircraft extended the range of the battlecruiser's armaments well beyond gun and visual range. As built, *Furious* was a hybrid battlecruiser/aircraft carrier. The Admiralty had identified the potential of aircraft as a reconnaissance and weapon-carrying system in 1912 when Lieutenant Samson piloted a Short S.27 seaplane from *Hibernia*, under way in Weymouth Bay. In 1913, a wireless-equipped Short S.64 seaplane took part in naval manoeuvres, and later that year a Sopwith seaplane flew with a torpedo slung between its floats.

War experience showed the need for aircraft-carrying ships to have a high speed in order for their aircraft to become airborne. In 1917, flying-off platforms were installed on top of gun turrets of cruisers and battlecruisers. In August 1917, a Sopwith Pup flown from the cruiser *Yarmouth* destroyed the Zeppelin *L23* near the Danish coast.

CONSTRUCTION

Invincible was built as a test bed for electric-powered gun turrets, rather than the tried hydraulic system. Despite exhaustive trials, the electric-powered turrets did not achieve the reliability and speed of operation of the hydraulic system. The electric system was changed to hydraulic during an eight-month refit in 1913–14.

The construction of the *Indefatigable* class was driven by the need to provide greater spacing between the two amidships turrets, P and Q. This allowed greater arcs of fire and enabled each to fire across deck in a broadside engagement without its blast adversely affecting the other gun turret. Additionally, the increase in the calibre of the 12-in. guns from 45 to 50 increased the diameter of the four gun turrets by 1ft (30.48cm) to 28ft (8.5m). An increase in hull length of 25ft (7.6m) over the *Invincible* class accommodated these changes. A and Y turrets were placed nearer to the ends of the ship, but this meant that the beam was 6ft (1.58m) less at these turret positions, than in the earlier ships.

The 'splendid cats' were the first battlecruisers with all centre-line main gun turrets, with the two fore gun turrets arranged with B turret superfiring over A. This required changes to the open sighting hoods on previous turrets to prevent the effects of blast injuring the turret crew. The two after turrets were positioned some distance apart, with Q turret located amidships. The rationale was to reduce the target area of the turrets, in that both turrets could not be knocked out at the same time. The result of this design was that the arc of fire for Q turret, located between the second and third funnels, was restricted to 240 degrees. The magazine serving Q turret was located between two boiler rooms and therefore required cooling equipment to maintain the cordite at a low and even temperature to prevent deterioration.

The belt armour protection for the *Lion* class was thicker than in both the *Invincible* and *Indefatigable* classes, and the vertical armour plate was carried a deck higher than in the previous classes. However, the

HMS *Queen Mary*, the only battlecruiser equipped with the Argo fire-control system. This 'crack gunnery ship' hit *Seydlitz* four times in the 'run to the south', before breaking in two between the foremast and forward funnel. (IWM)

depth of the armour plate below the waterline, at 3ft (91cm), was shown at the battle of Dogger Bank to be a weak point.

Queen Mary was laid down 16 months after *Lion* and differed slightly in terms of displacement, beam and ship horsepower. Whilst armed with the same mark of 13.5-in. guns, her mountings for these guns were modified to accommodate the loading of a heavier, 1,400lb (635kg), shell rather than the 1,250lb (570kg) shell carried by *Lion* and *Princess Royal*. *Queen Mary* had different fire-control arrangements from her sister ships. The main fire-control position was placed on top of the conning tower rather than the foremast, which carried a spotting top only. In addition, each gun turret was fitted with fire-control instruments to allow for local control of each turret by its gun captain. An Argo clock Mk IV, one of five sets ordered by the Admiralty to trial against the Dreyer table, was fitted and *Queen Mary* was the only battlecruiser fitted with this superior fire-control system. The Argo clock could calculate the range to the target's future position, even when the firing and target ship were rapidly changing course. Thus, *Queen Mary* gained her reputation as a 'crack gunnery ship'. She differed visually from her sister ships by the shape of her funnels, which were round, rather than oval.

Tiger's construction reflected a finalization of design issues that had arisen with the trials and operation of previous battlecruisers. Her double bottom was utilized for oil storage, which significantly increased her capacity for oil to feed her more powerful machinery and increased radius of action. The experience gained in fitting out the double bottom for oil storage provided valuable input for the design of the all-oil-fired dreadnoughts of the *Queen Elizabeth* class. The grouping together of her three funnels, with their increased height, overcame the smoke interference that occurred with earlier ships. The placement of Q turret astern of all the funnels increased the arc of fire from 240 degrees to 300 degrees. Additionally, placing Q turret on the forecastle deck allowed it to fire over X turret further astern. This layout reflected the design of the Japanese battlecruiser *Kongo* built in Britain and launched in May 1912, before *Tiger* was laid down.

The *Renown* class were the first all-oil-powered, 15-in. gunned, battlecruisers. In addition, with Fisher shaking up Admiralty design and ordering procedures, they were launched in just over a year and completed in less than two years. To achieve their high speed with 15-in. guns, the hull was 90ft (27.43m) longer than *Tiger* and 2,000 tons lighter in displacement. To cope with heavy weather in the North Sea, the ships had a flared bow

HMS *Furious* in 1918 after the removal of the aft gun turret and construction of a landing platform. The goal post arrestor system behind the single funnel is visible; however, turbulence from the bridge and funnel made aircraft landing problematic. (IWM)

and their two forward gun turrets were carried at a higher level. They carried three more boilers and the same machinery as in *Tiger*. The weight saving was achieved by returning to the level of armour protection of the *Invincible* class.

The *Courageous*-class ships were the first large ships to be fitted with geared turbines and small-tube boilers. These boilers generated an increase of 30 per cent in power compared with large-tube boilers of the same weight. Because of the limited availability of 15-in. gun turrets and guns, the *Courageous* class only carried four 15-in. guns in two turrets, one forward and one aft. Secondary armament was also 4-in. guns in triple mountings, with two mountings aft on the centre line and two mountings on each beam, one adjacent to the funnel and the other adjacent to the bridge. All mountings were carried on the shelter deck.

Construction of *Furious* commenced to the design carrying two 18-in. guns, and marked the next stage in the process of increasing gun size. During construction, the forward 18-in. gun turret was removed and a 160ft (49m) flying-off deck was built from forward of the conning tower to her bow. The flying-off deck had a declination of 7 degrees. A hangar was built beneath the flying-off deck and *Furious* could carry five Sopwith Pups and three Short 184 seaplanes. The latter were launched from a trolley that ran down rails fixed to the deck, with an arrestor system containing shock absorbers at the bow that stopped the trolley from going overboard as the seaplane became airborne.

Furious returned to Elswick in November 1917 for the aft 18-in. gun turret, torpedo control tower and mainmast to be removed. A 300ft (90m) landing platform and hangar were built aft from her funnel with two narrow 11ft (3.4m) strips built around each side of the funnel and bridge to connect to the flying-off deck. Both hangars were fitted with lifts and aircraft capacity increased to 22 planes. Arrestor ropes with sandbags were fitted to catch hooks on the Sopwith Pup's skid undercarriage, and a goalpost with vertical ropes acted as a safety barrier to prevent aircraft crashing into the funnel and bridge superstructure. *Furious* joined the Grand Fleet in March 1918. Whilst she was able to successfully launch aircraft, the airflow from the bridge, foremast and funnel when the ship was under way caused so much turbulence over the new landing platform that nine out of 13 attempts at landing resulted in crashes.

Battlecruiser development

The following table shows the development of the battlecruiser during the construction period 1906 to 1917.

BATTLECRUISER DEVELOPMENT

Name	Length	Displacement	Armour Protection	Main Armament	Speed
Furious	750ft (230m)	19,513 tons	Belt 3in. (7.6cm) Deck 1.75in. (4.5cm)	1 x 18-in.	31.5kt
Courageous	735ft (225m)	18,600 tons	Belt 3in. (7.6cm) Deck 1in. (2.5cm)	4 x 15-in.	32kt
Renown	750ft (230m)	26,500 tons	Belt 6in. (15cm) Deck 1.5in. (3.8cm)	6 x 15-in.	32.6kt
Tiger	660ft (200m)	28,500 tons	Belt 9in. (23cm) Deck 1.5in. (3.8cm)	8 x 13.5-in.	29kt(+)
Lion	660ft (200m)	26,350 tons	Belt 9in. (23cm) Deck 1in. (2.5cm)	8 x 13.5-in.	27kt(+)
Indefatigable	555ft (170m)	18,800 tons	Belt 6in. (15cm) Deck 1in. (2.5cm)	8 x 12-in.	25kt(+)
Invincible	530ft (160m)	17,250 tons	Belt 6in. (15cm) Deck 1in. (2.5cm)	8 x 12-in.	25kt(+)
Dreadnought	490ft (150m)	17,900 tons	Belt 11in. (28cm) Deck 0.75in. (1.9cm)	10 x 12-in.	21kt
Lord Nelson*	410ft (125m)	16,500 tons	Belt 12in. (30.5cm) Deck 1.5in. (3.8cm)	4 x 12-in.	18kt
Minotaur#	490ft (150m)	14,600 tons	Belt 6in. (15cm) Deck 2in. (5cm)	4 x 9.2-in.	23kt(-)

Note: * = pre-dreadnought battleship. # = pre-dreadnought armoured cruiser.

MODIFICATIONS

All battlecruisers were modified during their service life to incorporate new technology and weapons. These modifications were primarily: fire control, aircraft, secondary armaments, AA guns, searchlights and increased funnel height to decrease the impact of coal smoke.

SHIP LEGENDS:

Name	Builder	Laid down	Launched	Commissioned
Invincible	Elswick	April 1906	April 1907	March 1909
Indomitable	Fairfield	March 1906	March 1907	June 1908
Inflexible	Clydebank	February 1906	June 1907	January 1909

Dimensions:	530ft (160m) x 78.5ft (24m) x 25.5ft (7.8m) = 17,250 tons
Armament:	8 x 12-in./.45-cal.
	16 x 4-in./.45-cal.
	1 x 3-in.
	7 maxims
	5 x 18-in. submerged torpedo tubes
Fire-control system:	From 1912, Dreyer Table Mk 1 plus Vickers range clock
	Barr and Stroud 9ft (2.75m) rangefinder
Wireless set:	Mk II set on completion; later changes to Types 1 and 9
	Invincible's wireless was upgraded on her way to the Falklands with a Poulsen long-range wireless set transferred from Defence
Armour Protection:	Belt 6in. (15cm) to 4in. (10cm)
	Bulkhead 7in. (18cm) to 6in. (15cm)
	Barbettes 7in. (18cm) to 2in. (5cm)
	Turrets 7in. (18cm)
	Turret roof 3in. (7.6cm)
	Conning tower 10in. (25cm) and 6in. (15cm)
	Decks: Main 1.75in. (4.5cm)
	Lower 2.5in. (6.4cm), 2in. (5cm), 1.5in. (3.8cm)
	Magazine screens 2.5in. (6.4cm)

Machinery:	Parsons turbines rated at 45,000shp = 25kt
	4 screws
	31 Yarrow large-tube boilers
Fuel:	3,084 tons of coal, plus 725 tons of oil
Radius of action:	6,210nm at 10kt; 3,050nm at 22.3kt
Complement:	722; 1,032 as flagship at Jutland, 31 May 1916

HMS *New Zealand*, seen from the bridge of HMAS *Australia*. A Maori chief gave the captain a Tiki pendant and grass war skirt to wear, to save the ship from harm. (IWM)

SHIP LEGENDS:

Name	Builder	Laid down	Launched	Commissioned
Indefatigable	Devonport	February 1909	October 1909	February 1911
New Zealand	Fairfield	June 1910	July 1911	November 1912
Australia	J. Brown & Co	June 1910	October 1911	June 1913

Dimensions:	555ft (170m) x 80ft (24m) x 27ft (8.25m) = 18,800 tons
Armament:	8 x 12-in./.45-cal.
	16 x 4-in./.50-cal.
	4 x 3-pdr
	2 x 18-in. submerged torpedo tubes
Fire-control system:	From 1912, Dreyer Table Mk 1 plus Vickers range clock
	Barr and Stroud 9ft (2.75m) rangefinder
Wireless set:	Mk I W/T, W/T 9 short-radius
Armour Protection:	Belt 6in. (15cm) to 4in. (10cm)
	Bulkheads 4in. (10cm)
	Barbettes 7in. (18cm) to 3in. (7.6cm)
	Turrets 7in. (18cm)
	Turret roof 3in. (7.6cm)
	Conning tower 10in. (25cm)
	Communication tubes 4in. (10cm) to 3in. (7.6cm)
	Spotting tower 6in. (15cm)
	Magazine screens 2.5in. (6.4cm)
	Decks: Main 1in. (2.5cm)
	Lower 1in. (2.5cm)
	Fore and aft 2.5in. (6.4cm) over steering
	Funnel uptakes 1in. (2.5cm) to 1.5in. (3.8cm)
Machinery:	Parsons turbines rated at 44,000shp = 25kt
	4 screws
	31 Babcock and Wilcox large-tube boilers
Fuel:	3,170 tons of coal, plus 840 tons of oil
Radius of action:	6,690nm at 10kt; 3,360nm at 23.5kt
Complement:	800

SHIP LEGENDS:

Name	Builder	Laid down	Launched	Commissioned
Lion	Devonport	November 1909	August 1910	May 1912
Princess Royal	Vickers	May 1910	April 1911	November 1912
Queen Mary	Palmers	March 1911	March 1912	September 1913

Dimensions:	*Lion* and *Princess Royal* 660ft (200m) x 88.5ft (27m) x 26.5ft (8.1m) = 26,350 tons
	Queen Mary 660ft (200m) x 89ft (27.1m) x 26.5ft (8m.1) = 27,000 tons
Armament:	8 x 13.5-in./.45-cal.
	16 x 4-in./.50-cal.
	4 x 3pdr
	2 x 21-in. submerged torpedo tubes
	Queen Mary carried the heavier 1,400lb 13.5-in. shell
Fire-control system:	*Lion* and *Princess Royal* Dreyer Table Mk III plus Dreyer/Elphinstone clock
	Queen Mary Dreyer Table Mk II plus Argo clock Mk IV
	Barr and Stroud 9ft (2.75m) rangefinder
Wireless set:	Mk I, Mk II, Type 9 W/T short-radius
Armour Protection:	Belt 6in. (15cm) to 4in. (10cm)
	Bulkheads 4in. (10cm)
	Barbettes 9in. (23cm) to 3in. (7.6cm)
	Turrets 9in. (23cm)
	Turret roof 3.5in. (9cm)
	Conning tower 10in. (25cm)
	Signal tower 6in. (15cm)
	Communication tubes 4in. (10cm) to 3in. (7.6cm)
	Magazine screens 2.5in. (6.4cm) to 1in.
	Decks: Upper 1in. (2.5cm)
	Lower 1in. (2.5cm) to 1.25in. (3.2cm) with 2.5in. (6.4cm) ends over steering
	Funnel uptakes 1.5in. (3.8cm) to 1in. (2.5cm)
Machinery:	*Lion* and *Princess Royal* Parsons turbines rated at 70,000shp = 27kt
	4 screws
	Queen Mary Vickers turbines rated at 75,000shp = 27kt
	4 screws
	42 Yarrow large tube boilers
Fuel:	*Lion* and *Princess Royal* 3,500 tons of coal, plus 1,135 tons of oil
	Queen Mary 3,700 tons of coal, plus 1,130 tons of oil
Radius of action:	5,610nm at 10kt; 2,420nm at 23.9kt
Complement:	997

A stern port quarter view of HMS *Lion* in 1915, showing the 13.5-in. guns of X turret. (IWM)

SHIP LEGENDS:

Name	Builder	Laid down	Launched	Commissioned
Tiger	J. Brown & Co	June 1912	December 1913	October 1914

Aerial view of **HMAS** *Australia* showing foremast, rangefinder and training scale on A turret. **(IWM)**

Dimensions:	660ft (200m) x 90.5ft (27.6m) x 28.5ft (8.7m) = 28,500 tons
Armament:	8 x 13.5-in./.45-cal.
	12 x 4-in./.45-cal.
	4 x 3pdr
	2 x 3-in. AA
	4 x 21-in. submerged torpedo tubes
	5 Maxims
	10 Lewis guns
Fire-control system:	Dreyer Table Mk IV, with Dreyer Turret Control Table plus
	Dreyer/Elphinstone clock
	Barr and Stroud 9ft (2.75m) rangefinder
Wireless set:	Types 1–34
	Type 16
Armour Protection:	Belt 9in. (23cm) to 3in. (7.6cm)
	Bulkheads 4in. (10cm) to 2in. (5cm)
	Barbettes 9in. (23cm) to 1in. (2.5cm)
	Turrets 9in. (23cm)
	Turret roof 4.5in. (11.5cm)
	Secondary batteries 6in. (15cm)
	Conning tower 10in. (25cm)
	Communications tube 4in. (10cm) to 3in. (7.6cm)
	Torpedo control 6in. (15cm)
	Magazine screens 2.5in. (6.4cm)
	Decks: Forecastle 1.5in. (3.8cm)
	Upper 1.5in. (3.8cm)
	Main 1in. (2.5cm)
	Lower 3in. (7.6cm)
Machinery:	Brown Curtis impulse turbines rated at 108,000hp = 29kt
	4 screws
	39 Babcock and Wilcox boilers
Fuel:	3,480 tons of coal, plus 3,480 tons of oil
Radius of action:	5,200nm at 12kt; 2,800nm at 25kt
Complement:	1,121 September 1914; 1,459 April 1918.

SHIP LEGENDS:

Name	Builder	Laid down	Launched	Commissioned
Renown	Fairfield Co.	January 1915	March 1916	September 1916
Repulse	J. Brown & Co	January 1915	January 1916	August 1916

Dimensions:	750ft (230m) x 90ft (27.5m) x 27.5ft (8.4m) = 26,500 tons
Armament:	6 x 15-in./.42-cal.
	17 x 4-in./.44-cal.
	2 x 3-in. AA 4 x 3pdr
	2 x 21-in. submerged torpedo tubes
	5 Maxim guns
Fire-control system:	Dreyer Table Mk IV and Dreyer Turret Control Table plus
	Dreyer/Elphinstone clock
	Barr and Stroud 15ft (4.6m) rangefinder
Wireless set:	Types 1–16
Armour Protection:	Belt 6in. (15cm) to 1.5in. (3.8cm)
	Barbettes 7in. (18cm) to 4in. (10cm)
	Turrets 11in. (30cm)
	Turret roof 4.25in. (10.8cm)
	Conning tower 10in. (25cm)
	Communication tubes 3in. (7.6cm)
	Decks: Forecastle 1.5in. (3.8cm)
	Upper 0.5in. (1.25cm)
	Main 3in. (7.6cm)
	Lower 2.5in. (6.4cm), over steering 3.5in. (9cm)
Machinery:	Brown Curtis turbines rated at 120,000shp = 32.6kt
	4 screws
	42 Babcock and Wilcox large-tube boilers
Fuel:	4,243 tons of oil
Radius of action:	4,700nm at 12 kt; 2,700nm at 25kt
Complement:	967

Name	Builder	Laid down	Launched	Commissioned
Courageous	Elswick	March 1915	February 1916	January 1917
Glorious	Harland & Wolf	March 1915	April 1916	January 1917

Dimensions:	735ft (225m) x 81ft (24.7m) x 23.25ft (7.1m) = 18,600 tons
Armament:	4 x 15-in. 18 x 4-in.
	2 x 3-in. HA
	2 x 21-in. submerged torpedo tubes
Fire-control system:	Dreyer Table Mk IV and Dreyer Turret Control Table
	plus Dreyer/Elphinstone clock
	Barr and Stroud 15ft (4.6m) rangefinder
Wireless set:	Types 1–16
Armour Protection:	Belt 3in. (7.6cm) to 2in. (5cm)
	Bulkheads 3in. (7.6cm) to 2in. (5cm)
	Barbettes 7in. (18cm) to 3in. (7.6cm)
	Turrets 9in. (23cm)
	Turret roof 4.25in. (10.8cm)
	Conning tower 10in. (25cm)
	Decks: Forecastle 1in. (2.5cm)
	Upper 1in. (2.5cm)
	Main 1.75in. (4.5cm)
	Lower 1.5in. (3.8cm), over steering 3in. (7.6cm)
Machinery:	Parsons all-geared turbines rated at 90,000shp = 32kt
	4 screws
	18 Yarrow small tube boilers
Fuel:	3,160 tons of oil
Radius of action:	6,000nm at 20kt
Complement:	842

A Sopwith aircraft being hoisted on board HMAS *Australia*. The flying-off platform over the 12-in. gun turret is seen, with the Forth Bridge in the background. (IWM)

Name	Builder	Laid down	Launched	Commissioned
Furious	Elswick	June 1915	August 1916	July 1917

Dimensions:	750ft (230m) x 88ft (27m) x 19.75ft (6m) = 19,513 tons
Armament:	2 x 18-in. as designed, but 1 x 18-in./.40-cal. as constructed
	11 x 5.5-in. 2 x 3-in. HA
	4 x 3-pdr
	4 x 21-in. above water and 2 x 21-in. submerged torpedo tubes
	As constructed: 5 Sopwith Pups
	3 Short 184 seaplanes
	After November 1917 conversion: 14 Sopwith 1.5 strutters
	8 Sopwith 2F.1 Camels
Fire-control system:	Dreyer Table Mk IV and Dreyer Turret Control Table plus
	Dreyer/Elphinstone clock
	Barr and Stroud 15ft (4.6m) rangefinder
Wireless set:	Types 1–16
Armour Protection:	Sides 2in. (5cm) to 3in. (7.6cm) armour over 1in. (2.5cm) plating
	Bulkheads 2in. (5cm) to 3in. (7.6cm)
	Barbette 7in. (18cm)
	Turret 13in. (33cm)
	Turret roof 4.5in. (11.5cm)
	Conning tower 10in. (25cm)
	Decks: Forecastle 1in. (25cm)
	Upper 1in. (25cm)
	Main between barbettes 1.75in. (4.5cm)
	Lower 1.5in. (3.8cm) with 3in. (7.6cm) over steering
Machinery:	Brown-Curtis geared turbines rated at 94,000shp = 31.5kt
	4 screws
	18 Yarrow small tube boilers
Fuel:	3,160 tons of oil
Radius of action:	6,000nm at 20kt
Complement:	880 as an aircraft carrier

BATTLECRUISERS AT WAR

Within five months of the beginning of the war, British battlecruisers had marked a significant strategic point in the naval war. Britain's command of the sea was absolute. Between them *Invincible, Inflexible, Indomitable, Indefatigable, Princess Royal* and *Australia*, with their light forces, had swept the oceans clean of German merchant and naval ships. This allowed the Canadian, Indian and ANZAC troop convoys to safely land their armies and for Britain to trade with the world for the foodstuffs and war materials she needed to execute the war. *Australia* had provided naval support for the capture and occupation of Germany's South Pacific colonies. Fisher's concept for the strategic role and global operations of the battlecruiser had been fulfilled.

The more dramatic actions in which battlecruisers took part were as follows.

Heligoland Bight

The first action in which British battlecruisers fired their guns in anger was the Heligoland Bight action on 28 August 1914. This was a well-conceived plan to 'assert command of the North Sea right up to the enemy gates' by intercepting, at dawn, German torpedo boats commencing their day patrols north of Heligoland Island. The Harwich Force of two light cruisers and 33 destroyers was to be the attacking force, with *Invincible* and *New Zealand* in support.

The planning by the Admiralty War Staff, whose role was to provide a centralized direction to naval operations, was poor. This resulted in significant confusion between the commanders in action and, with German forces arriving in superior strength, upset the plan's objective. A heavy sea mist with fog banks reduced visibility, adding to the confusion. The Harwich Force, after some initial successes, had to withdraw under serious threat from German light cruisers. Fortunately, Admiral Jellicoe, who had not been informed of the operation until the Harwich Force sailed, ordered Admiral Beatty and his battlecruisers and light cruisers to join the two battlecruisers to provide support.

As the hard-pressed Harwich Force withdrew they called for support, which was provided at first by the 1st Light Cruiser Squadron, and the German cruiser *Mainz* was sunk. As more German cruisers joined the action additional support was requested. Beatty had to decide to risk his five battlecruisers in an area, within 25 miles (40km) of the main German naval base, that might have been mined and where submarines might have been on patrol. Additionally, the weather remained misty, reducing visibility to mere miles. Notwithstanding these risks, Beatty led the five battlecruisers, *Lion*, *Queen Mary*, *Princess Royal*, *New Zealand* and *Invincible*, south-east into the Heligoland Bight at 25 knots.

Lion sighted the German cruiser *Köln*, and opened fire at 7,800 yards (7,100m), with the range reducing to 6,500 yards (5,900m). The *Köln* remained in sight of *Lion* and her consorts for seven minutes and was repeatedly hit before disappearing into a fog bank. Another German cruiser, *Ariadne*, appeared out of the fog on *Lion*'s port bow at 7,000 yards (6,400m) and in the space of a few minutes was reduced to a flaming wreck. *Invincible*, at the end of the battlecruiser line and 2 miles (3.2km) behind *Lion*, left the battle line and followed *Köln* to the north-east and opened fire on her at a range of 5,000 yards (4,600m). *Invincible* fired 18 12-in. shells at *Köln* without securing a hit. Beatty led his battlecruisers to the north to locate the *Köln*, which was sighted at a range of 4,000 yards (3,650m), and subjected her to a further barrage from the battlecruisers which reduced her to a sinking hulk. Beatty then withdrew his forces, and the Harwich Force, from the Bight.

The Heligoland Bight action was seen in Britain as a great success. Three German light cruisers, *Mainz*, *Köln* and *Ariadne*, and a torpedo boat, *V-187*, had been sunk on the doorstep of the High Seas Fleet. For the German Navy, the effect on morale was bad as the action reinforced the assertive and aggressive reputation of the Royal Navy. The Kaiser gave orders restricting the opportunities for operations of the High Seas Fleet, and the range that it could sail from port. This reinforced its role as a 'fleet in being' tethered to its anchorage.

HMS *Inflexible*'s A gun turret opening fire at the battle of the Falklands. (IWM)

The search for the German East Asia Squadron

When war was declared, the German East Asia Squadron, comprising the armoured cruisers *Scharnhorst* and *Gneisenau* and the light cruisers *Emden*, *Leipzig*, *Nürnberg* and *Dresden*, was on a

HMS *Inflexible* during the battle of the Falklands. *Inflexible* switched off the Dreyer fire-control system during the battle as it could not cope with the rapid changes in range. (IWM)

training cruise in the Pacific's Caroline Islands. Unable to return to his base at Tsingtao, Admiral von Spee took his squadron across the Pacific to the South American coast to avoid HMAS *Australia*, under the command of Admiral Patey. The light cruiser *Emden* was detached to operate as a commerce raider in the Indian Ocean, until destroyed by HMAS *Sydney* on 9 November 1914.

In searching for von Spee, *Australia* criss-crossed the south-eastern Pacific, and provided naval support for the capture and occupation of the German South Pacific colonies of New Guinea, Rabaul, the Bismarck Archipelago, the Solomons and Samoa. When Admiral Patey finally had intelligence that von Spee was heading for South America, *Australia* followed.

The sinking of Admiral Cradock's two armoured cruisers, *Good Hope* and *Monmouth*, at Coronel on 1 November 1914 by von Spee followed by days the reappointment of Admiral Fisher as First Sea Lord. Within hours of the news of the defeat at Coronel reaching the Admiralty on 4 November Fisher ordered *Invincible* and *Inflexible* to sail for the Falklands under the command of Admiral Sturdee. *Princess Royal* was ordered to join the West Indies Squadron to guard the Caribbean from von Spee coming through the Panama Canal.

Sturdee and his command arrived at the Falklands on 7 December 1914, and were still coaling when von Spee's ships *Gneisenau* and *Nürnberg* were spotted approaching the island on the morning of 8 December. A practice shell fired by *Canopus*, a pre-dreadnought battleship that had been grounded in the harbour as a defensive measure, fell short, ricocheted and hit one of *Gneisenau*'s funnels. This caused *Gneisenau* to steer away from the island, and gave Sturdee sufficient time to clear his ships from the anchorage and give chase to von Spee's fleeing squadron. However, the superior speed and armament of *Invincible* and *Inflexible* enabled them to bring *Scharnhorst* and *Gneisenau* within the 16,400-yard (15,000m) range of their 12-in. guns, but stay outside the 13,500-yard (12,350m) range of von Spee's 8.2-in. guns.

The battle of the Falklands lasted from 1pm, when *Inflexible* opened fire at 16,000 yards (14,600m), until 6pm, when *Gneisenau* finally sank. The battle was characterized by a long chase, followed by the enemy's continual zigzagging and Sturdee's frequent changes in course to remain out of range of the enemy's guns. Neither *Invincible* nor *Inflexible* suffered any significant casualties or damage. Sturdee fought the battle in accordance with Fisher's concept for the battlecruiser. The battlecruisers fired 1,174 rounds in sinking the *Scharnhorst* and *Gneisenau*. Although *Invincible* had a gun director fitted, it was not operational at the time of the battle. Both *Invincible* and *Inflexible* used turret control for aiming and firing, which was subject to interference both by funnel smoke and sea spray. The Dreyer fire-control system could not cope with the frequent changes in range and was switched off. Another major factor was that their 12-in. shells were passing right through the German armoured cruisers without exploding. Although the *Gneisenau* suffered at least 50 direct hits, her sinking was aided by scuttling charges. The light cruisers *Leipzig* and *Nürnberg* were also sunk, with the *Dresden* managing to escape. She was sunk in March 1915, by *Glasgow*.

Invincible and *Inflexible* sailed for Britain on 16 December, and both ships refitted at Gibraltar in January 1915. *Inflexible* was ordered to the Dardanelles, where she arrived on 24 January to replace *Indefatigable*, which sailed to Malta for a refit prior to joining the Grand Fleet. *Australia*, having sailed across the Pacific, continued through the Magellan Straits and coaled at the Falklands. On route to Britain, *Australia* sank the *Eleanore Woermann*, a coal supply ship for von Spee's squadron, and finally arrived at Plymouth on 29 January 1915 for a needed refit, having sailed from Sydney on 2 August 1914.

HMS *Tiger*. Battlecruisers emitted vast amounts of thick coal smoke that quickly reduced visibility and interfered with spotting the target. (IWM)

The battle of Dogger Bank

On 23 January 1915, Room 40, the secret signals intercept and decrypt operation, intercepted and read von Ingenohl's order to Hipper to conduct a reconnaissance of the Dogger Bank. Room 40 were able to determine the timing, objective, area of operation and force structure, and this allowed the Admiralty War Staff to determine a time and interception point 30 miles (48km) north of the Dogger Bank, which led to the first clash of battlecruisers.

Beatty with *Lion*, *Tiger* and *Princess Royal* as the 1st Battlecruiser Squadron, and *New Zealand* and *Indomitable* as the newly formed 2nd Battlecruiser Squadron, under the command of Admiral Moore, with light cruisers, were to rendezvous with Commodore Tyrwhitt and the Harwich Force of three light cruisers and 35 destroyers at 7am on 24 January.

At 7.20am *Aurora*, a Harwich Force light cruiser, spotted and engaged a light cruiser of Hipper's force. The two battlecruiser forces sighted each other at 8.40am, and Hipper with the *Seydlitz*, *Moltke*, *Derfflinger* and the armoured cruiser *Blücher* turned for home. The day was clear with only the horizon limiting visibility, and the sea was calm. Hipper was restrained by the lower speed, 23 knots, of *Blücher* and the higher speed of Beatty's battlecruisers allowed him slowly to overhaul the fleeing Germans.

Just before 9am, *Lion* opened a slow and deliberate fire on *Blücher*, the rear ship, at a range of 20,000 yards (18,300m). At 9.14am *Lion* shifted fire to the next in line, *Derfflinger*, with *Tiger* and *Princess Royal* opening fire on *Blücher*. As the battle progressed, Beatty was able to bring all the German battlecruisers under fire at a range of 17,500 yards (16,000m), although *Tiger* misunderstood a target distribution signal from *Lion* and fired on Hipper's leading ship, *Seydlitz*, along with *Lion*, leaving *Moltke* unengaged. The German battlecruisers concentrated fire on *Lion*, which was hit 17 times during the course of the battle, but her main armour belt was not penetrated. *Tiger* was hit six times, with her Q turret being put out of action. Hits on *Tiger's* main armour belt did not penetrate.

The cumulative effects of hits on *Lion's* hull displaced an armoured plate, causing flooding of the boiler feed tanks. Contamination with salt water eventually stopped her engines. As *Lion* withdrew from the battle

A: HMS *Indefatigable*

A

B: HMS *Lion*, 31 May 1916

B

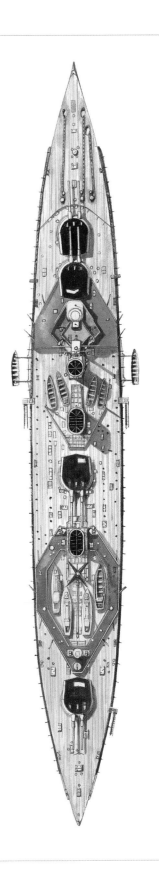

D: HMS *INVINCIBLE*

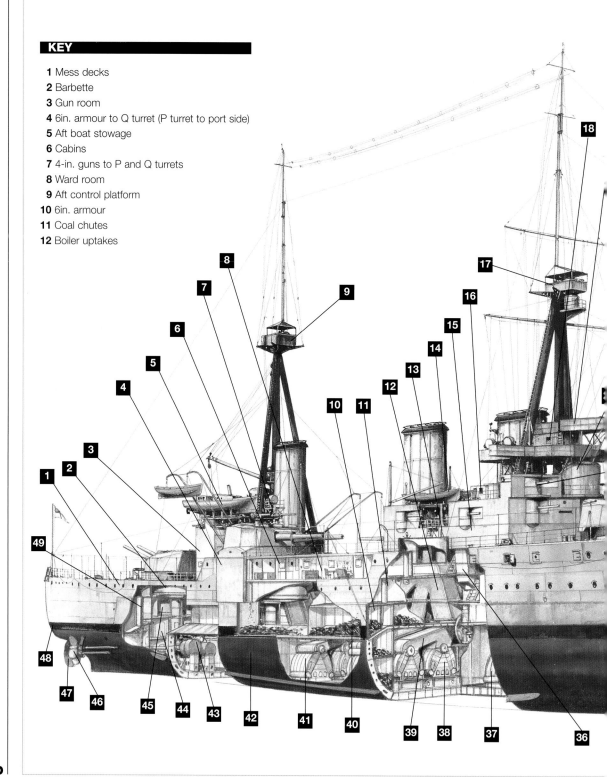

D

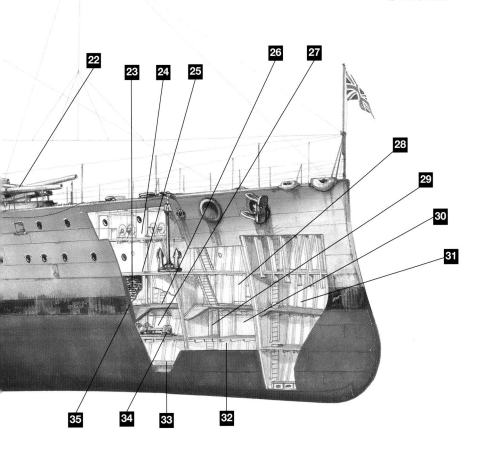

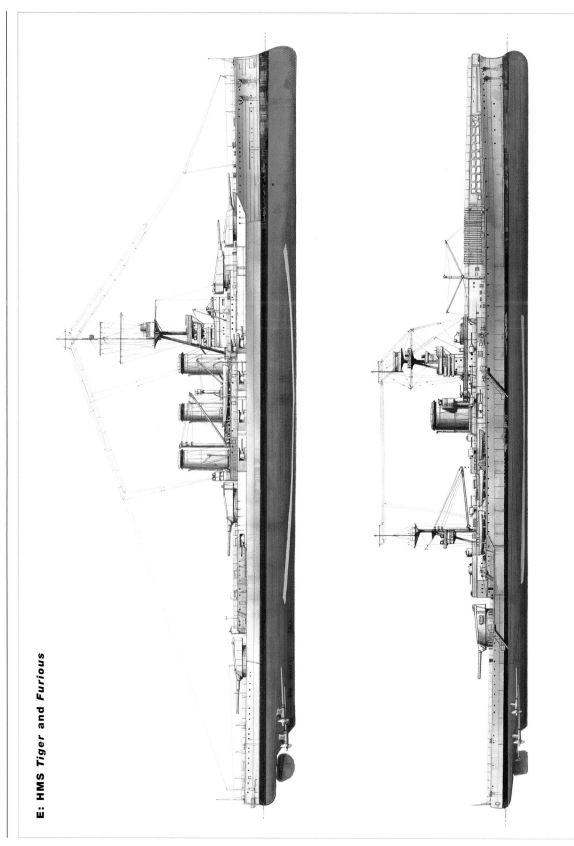

E: HMS *Tiger and* *Furious*

F: Wreck of HMS *Invincible*

G: Magazine and ammunition passageways on HMS *Queen Mary*

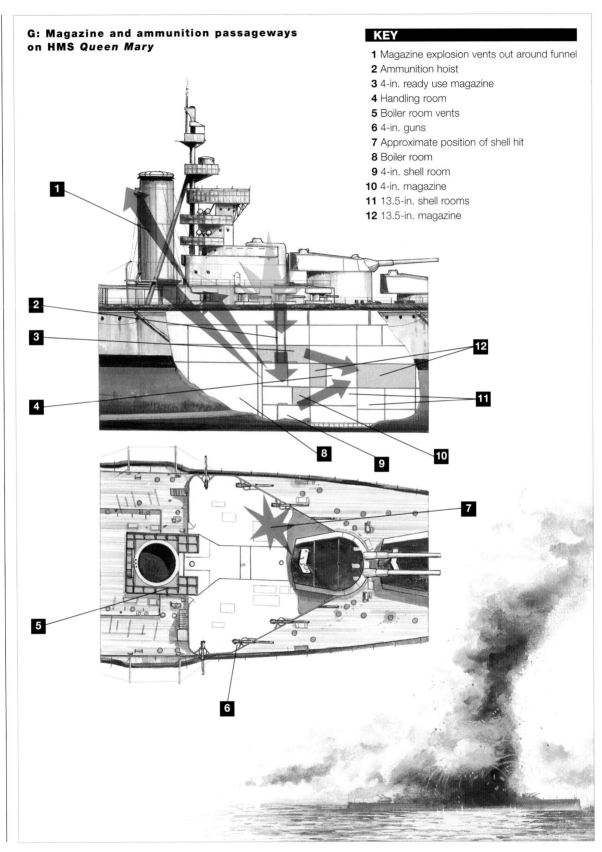

at 11am, Beatty's signal to his command for them to close the range to
Hipper's battlecruisers was read as part of another of his course change
signals, with the result that his remaining battlecruisers gave up the
chase to concentrate on the disabled *Blücher* and sink her. Hipper left
Blücher to her fate and escaped.

Lion had inflicted serious damage on Hipper's flagship, the *Seydlitz*.
At 9.50am a shell from *Lion* struck *Seydlitz*'s quarter-deck and penetrated
the armoured barbette of the aft turret. The explosion ignited cordite
propellant charges in the working chamber which flashed down to the
magazine handling room as well as up to the turret killing all the crew. An
opened door, connecting the aft barbette to the adjoining superimposed
turret, allowed the flames to reach into this structure, igniting more
cordite propellant charges, burning out this turret and killing the crew as
well. The magazines for both turrets were flooded, preventing the loss of
the ship. In all, 62 cordite charges ignited. In addition to this hit the
Seydlitz was only hit once more, with the *Derfflinger* also only suffering one
hit. The *Blücher* was hit many times but continued to fight until two
torpedoes caused her to capsize and sink.

Whilst the battle of Dogger Bank was seen by the British public as a
victory, the escape of Hipper's battlecruisers was a great disappointment.
Although telling hits were made at 17,500 yards (16,000m), excluding the
hits on *Blücher*, gunnery results were seen as very unsatisfactory. Only *Tiger*
had a gun director fitted, but she overestimated the range and confused
her shooting with the splashes of *Lion*. The Dreyer fire-control system was
shown to be inadequate to the task. Unfortunately, *Queen Mary*, with the
superior Argo fire-control system was absent from the battle, undergoing a
refit. Moore, who assumed command of the battlecruisers when *Lion* with
Beatty on board withdrew from the battle line, was severely criticized for
not continuing the chase and was transferred to another command.

For the Germans, the loss of the *Blücher* resulted in Admiral von
Ingenohl losing his command of the High Seas Fleet, which was restricted
in sailing not more than 120 miles (193km) from Heligoland. The hit
on *Seydlitz*'s aft turret subsequently led to anti-flash equipment being
introduced to all German capital ships and, more importantly, a reduction
in the number of cordite charges held outside the magazine during action.

The second Dardanelles bombardment

Inflexible took part in the bombardment of the outer forts of the Dardanelles
on 19 and 25 February and 4 and 5 March 1915. After changing the
worn-out guns of A turret at Malta, *Inflexible* was back on station by 17
March. On 18 March, a bombardment of the inner forts of the Dardanelles

Straits took place to suppress their fire so minesweepers could clear the minefields within the Straits and enable the fleet to sail through to Constantinople.

Inflexible hit Fort Rumeli Hamidieh, putting two 14-in. guns out of action. However, the bombarding ships faced a total of 57 guns, including 32 mobile howitzers. *Inflexible* was hit by six shells, with one hitting the roof of the foretop, mortally wounding the spotting crew. As *Inflexible* withdrew from her position 6 miles (9.5km) inside the Straits at 4.11pm, she hit a mine on her starboard bow adjacent to the torpedo flat, killing 27 crew members, and suffered a hole 15ft x 15ft (4.6m x 4.6m). Following repairs, *Inflexible* joined the Battlecruiser Fleet.

The battle of Jutland

The battle of Jutland occurred on the afternoon of 31 May 1916. It represents the largest clash of battleships in history and the only clash of dreadnoughts during the First World War. It involved 251 ships from the Grand Fleet and the High Seas Fleet dashing across the sea, adding vast amounts of thick dark coal smoke to patches of sea mist and blotting out visibility for both sides. With the exception of the 5th Battle Squadron (5BS), no dreadnought saw an adversary for more than a few minutes. In what was an increasingly confusing situation and devoid of consistent and accurate intelligence, the commanders on both sides, Admirals Jellicoe and Scheer, had to make split-second tactical decisions that had far-reaching strategic results. This description of the battle will only cover the battlecruiser involvement.

Room 40 determined that a major operation by the Germans was imminent through decoding and analysing a series of German wireless messages. As a consequence Jellicoe was ordered to sail on the night of 30 May, before the High Seas Fleet left its anchorage. Beatty's battlecruisers, *Lion, Princess Royal, Queen Mary, Tiger, New Zealand* and *Indefatigable*, were ordered to rendezvous with Jellicoe off the entrance to the Skaggerak. The 3rd Battlecruiser Squadron (3BCS), under the command of Admiral Hood, sailed from Scapa Flow, where it had been engaged in gunnery practice, with the Grand Fleet. Its position within the Battlecruiser Fleet had been temporarily replaced by 5BS, under the command of Rear Admiral Evan-Thomas, comprising the new fast 15-in. gunned dreadnoughts, *Barham, Valiant, Warspite* and *Malaya*. *Australia* was absent from the fleet, in dock for repairs.

A Danish tramp steamer, *N. J. Fjord*, had sailed from Leith, downriver from the battlecruiser anchorage at Rosyth on 29 May, with a cargo of coal for the Danish east-coast port of Friedrickshaven. *Galatea*, a screening light cruiser, spotted *N. J. Fjord* at 2.10pm on 31 May, blowing off steam as she was stopped by two German torpedo boats, part of Hipper's screen. At 2.32pm Beatty signalled to his fleet to turn so as to get between Hipper and his base, but this was not acted upon by 5th Battle Squadron (5BS) until the signal was repeated at 2.40pm. Consequently the distance between the 5BS flagship *Barham* and the *Lion* opened out to 10 miles (16km) and resulted in a 23-minute delay before *Barham* could join the battle.

HMS *Lion* after Jutland with the damaged Q turret removed. HMS *Lion* remained on active duty until a new gun turret was available for her. (IWM)

In the 50-minute period between *Barham* turning and *Lion* sighting Hipper's battlecruisers at 3.30pm, Beatty did not concentrate his ships together into line of battle and create the powerful fleet that on paper it represented. Additionally, Beatty's scouting forces, with the exception of the 2nd Light Cruiser Squadron (2LCS), left their positions to join *Galatea* in the action against Hipper's light forces. Beatty, therefore, had no intelligence as to the position and course of Hipper's battlecruisers, which appeared without prior warning to the east off *Lion's* starboard bow at a distance of 28,000 yards (25,600m) and sailing northwards. The weather was clear, with a little haze, and the sea was calm.

Hipper, on sighting Beatty, turned his new flagship, *Lützow*, on a south-easterly course, followed by *Derfflinger, Seydlitz, Moltke* and *Von der Tann*, to draw Beatty onto Scheer, who was sailing northwards towards them. Both Jellicoe and Beatty were unaware that the Germans were at sea. This was a result of bad communication by a War Staff officer with Room 40. Beatty steered easterly to close Hipper and gradually altered course to the south as his 'T' was being crossed.

Hipper enjoyed a period between sighting Beatty and opening fire to steady his course, order fire distribution and take rangefinder readings. In the same period Beatty had to order the line of battle formation, continually alter course and order line of bearing to clear following ships from funnel and gun smoke from preceding ships. These actions resulted in Beatty giving up the superior range of his 13.5-in. guns, and allowed Hipper to bring Beatty within his gun range and open fire first at 3.47pm. Although Beatty opened fire within a minute of Hipper, only the forward turrets of his ships could bear on the enemy.

The opening of gunfire marked the 'run to the south' phase of the battle. Whilst visibility was good, Beatty's battlecruisers were silhouetted against a clear western horizon and Hipper against a low-cloud, hazy horizon. Although both sides initially overestimated the range, the stereoscopic rangefinders of the German battlecruisers established an accurate range of 16,000 yards (14,650m) more quickly than the British Barr and Stroud coincidence rangefinders.

Beatty's failure to concentrate his forces and the continual course changes now began to tell as his battlecruisers suffered 14 hits between 3.47pm and 4.08pm, and only made three in reply. *Lion* suffered a hit on her Q turret which blew off the roof. Warrant Officer Grant's reorganization of *Lion's* ammunition-handling system in 1915 (see pp.39–42), and the prompt flooding of the magazine, kept the ship from blowing up. As it was, the cordite in the ammunition trunk provided a funeral pyre for the 80 crew members of Q turret. At 4.02pm *Von der Tann* hit *Indefatigable* with two salvos. The first salvo hit astern and *Indefatigable* began to keel over to port and sink by the stern. The second salvo hit near A turret and, after an appreciable pause, *Indefatigable* blew up. *Queen Mary* was responsible for two of the three British hits on *Seydlitz*, one of which burnt out the aft superfiring turret, but as at Dogger Bank, *Seydlitz* did not blow up.

At 4.10pm, 23 minutes after *Lion* opened fire, *Barham* opened fire with her 15-in. guns at a range of 19,000 yards (17,400m), hitting *Von der Tann* at 4.11pm. The ships of 5BS were fitted with 15ft (4.6m) Barr and Stroud rangefinders and were on a steady course in line of battle and not troubled by either funnel smoke or gunfire from the preceding battlecruisers. Without the need to constantly manoeuvre to escape German shelling, the 5BS were able to achieve six hits on Hipper's battlecruisers as follows: *Von der Tann* – 1; *Moltke* – 4; *Seydlitz* – 1.

At 4.26pm *Queen Mary* blew up and sank – she had been engaged in a fierce dual with *Seydlitz*, with both ships hitting one another. At 4.20pm on *Lion*'s bridge a misunderstood helm order resulted in *Lion* veering out of line away from the enemy. *Derfflinger* followed fire distribution orders and shifted target from *Princess Royal* to the next ship in line, *Queen Mary*. *Derfflinger* timed her gunfire to alternate with *Seydlitz*, so *Queen Mary*

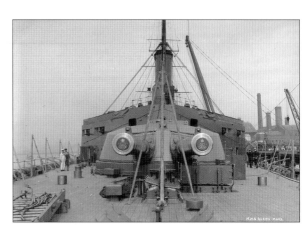

The quarter-deck and X turret of HMS *Queen Mary*. Four 4-in. guns of the stern secondary battery are visible above and to the left and right of X turret. (IWM)

was subject to a hail of shells from 4.22pm onwards. Two shells hit forward and an explosion vented from the boiler room ventilation hatches around the forward funnel directly behind the foremast, breaking the ship in two. Beatty, seeing the massive cloud of smoke from the explosion, said, 'There seems to be something wrong with our bloody ships today.'

Dublin, the fourth ship in line of Commodore Goodenough's 2LCS, was on the disengaged side of *Queen Mary*. William Cave of *Dublin* saw the forepart of *Queen Mary* largely intact.

> 'In every detail we could see officers and signalmen with others as the ship, already doing twenty knots with the fore section blown forward, causing a higher bow wave than before only listing slightly to Port, then skidding round to starboard towards *Dublin*. We actually ported our helm to avoid her hitting us but it proved unnecessary; with increasing list she dived, her fore turret guns at full elevation hot with firing, giving off a loud hissing as they met the water. It was terrible to see those poor souls so near yet so far and being unable to help.'

Midshipman Owen emerged from *Queen Mary*'s aft X turret and

> 'found the ship lying on her side. She was broken amidships, her bows were sticking up in the air and the stern was also sticking up out at an angle of about 45 degrees from the water … A few moments afterwards a tremendous explosion occurred in the forepart of the vessel, which must have blown the bows to atoms.'

Midshipman Storey emerged from the midships Q turret.

> 'When I arrived on top of the turret the foremost part of the ship was no more and you could see where the ship had broken off just by the foremast. The stern was coming rapidly up out of the water and the amidships portion was going down in the water. The two after funnels were lying down, the amidships funnel beside "Q" Turret, and we climbed over the debris and had just got down to the waters edge, when the after magazine "X" Turret blew up and blew us into the water, a salvo of shells having gone into the after magazine.'

At 4.30pm Commodore Goodenough on *Southampton*, leading the 2LCS 2 miles (3.25km) ahead of *Lion*, spotted the High Seas Fleet sailing towards them. Goodenough reported his sighting to Beatty and Jellicoe. At 4.40pm Beatty turned his battered battlecruisers and sailed north towards Jellicoe. In the space of 52 minutes Beatty had lost two battlecruisers to cataclysmic explosions and his superior six to five numbers had been reduced to four to five. Hipper's objective of trapping Beatty between himself and Scheer had, however, failed. Hipper's battlecruisers had proven gunfire superiority, registering 42 hits on Beatty's battlecruisers whilst only receiving 11 in return. The 5BS, in a shorter period and at longer ranges, registered six hits on Hipper, suffering only two in reply.

Beatty's course north pursued by 16 dreadnoughts and five battle-cruisers is referred to as the 'run to the north'. As Beatty turned his battlecruisers to the north, the 5BS was 8 miles (13km) away sailing towards him and the German Fleet. Beatty waited until the 5BS was adjacent to him before ordering it to turn to the north, which it did at 4.54pm. As a result, the 5BS was between Beatty's battlecruisers and Scheer and received a hail of fire when it turned north. Beatty used his superior speed to pull away from the High Seas Fleet and the 5BS fought off both German dreadnoughts and battlecruisers from 4.54pm until 6pm. The 5BS registered 13 hits on battlecruisers and five hits on dreadnoughts and suffered 13 hits in reply; Beatty's battlecruisers registered one hit but suffered five in reply during this period.

Beatty was heading to join Jellicoe, and steered towards the north-east. From the German viewpoint, Beatty was steering away from his base in Scotland, which would have been to the north-west, and steering for the northern tip of Denmark. However, the thought of sinking ships of the 5BS was a prize that Scheer and Hipper couldn't refuse and they blindly followed Beatty.

At 5.33pm Beatty's advance screen of light cruisers sighted *Black Prince*, one of Jellicoe's advance screen of armoured cruisers. Beatty swung his battlecruisers to the east, re-engaging Hipper's battlecruisers on his starboard beam and forcing them to turn to the east, towards Denmark. Beatty used his high speed to outflank Hipper. At 5.36pm the 3BCS, seeking to link up with Beatty and steering south-east, encountered and engaged three light cruisers of Hipper's advance force, disabling the *Wiesbaden* and damaging both *Pillau* and *Frankfurt*. As a result, Hipper circled his battlecruisers to his starboard to fall back on Scheer and was prevented from sighting the advancing Grand Fleet and warning Scheer, who continued gradually and blithely to steer further east.

At 5.56pm Beatty sighted the starboard column of Jellicoe's dread-noughts, which was advancing south-east in its anti-submarine cruising formation of six columns of four ships in line. At 6.01pm Beatty and Jellicoe were in visual touch. Beatty steamed eastwards across the front of Jellicoe's dreadnoughts and for the first time, at 6.14pm, Beatty advised Jellicoe of the location of Scheer. At 6.16pm Jellicoe deployed his 24 dreadnoughts into line of battle on his port, eastern-most column steering southeast. This deployment created an inverted letter 'L' with Hipper and Scheer sailing into the joining point, or elbow, of the two lines. Jellicoe's deployment, Beatty's outflanking manoeuvre and the timely intervention of the 3BCS, forcing Hipper to circle, gave the British ships the advantage of visibility for rangefinding. During the afternoon the visibility had deteriorated from the opening sightings of 24,000 yards (22,000m) to approximately 10,000 yards (9,150m), with the better visibility to the west as ships were silhouetted by the setting sun. Visibility to the east was patchy.

Q turret magazine exploding on HMS *Invincible*. Flame is also emerging from A turret. Commander Dannreuther in the spotting top on the foremast stepped into the sea and survived. Gasson, operating the Q turret rangefinder, was blown out and miraculously survived. (IWM)

The 3BCS, steering north-west, sighted Beatty advancing towards them, circled to take up a position to lead Beatty's battlecruisers. As 3BCS settled on its new south-east course, it sighted Hipper's battlecruisers to its south-west on the ships' starboard beam and opened fire at 6.23pm at a range of 9,000 yards (8,200m). The gunnery practice at Scapa paid dividends with *Invincible* hitting *Lützow* eight times in eight minutes. *Derfflinger* was hit three times and *Seydlitz* once. Hood called out through a voicepipe to Commander Dannreuther, *Invincible*'s gunnery officer, located in the foretop, 'Your fire is very good. Keep at it as quickly as you can.' Four hits on *Lützow* by *Invincible* struck the port bow by the broadside torpedo flat and resulted in significant flooding, which caused the *Lützow* to withdraw from the battle and eventually sink. Hipper had to transfer his flag to an accompanying torpedo boat.

At the commencement of the engagement, Hipper's battlecruisers could not see the 3BCS through the mist. Just before 6.30pm, the mist cleared and *Invincible* was clearly sighted by several of Hipper's ships. A shell struck *Invincible*'s Q midships turret, blew off the face plate and roof and exploded over the 12-in. guns. The port gun was being loaded; the cordite ignited and the flash reached down through the working chamber and ammunition hoist to the handling room, where a stack of unprotected cordite charges lay outside the open magazine door. This cordite exploded and blew through to P turret magazine, which also exploded, cutting the ship in two. The exploding midships magazines blew red-hot fragments through the large spaces of the engine room aft and the boiler rooms forward to reach both A and X turret magazines, which also exploded. The two halves of the world's first battlecruiser rested on the sea bottom with the bow and stern projecting above the sea before finally sinking. Commander Dannreuther and five other men survived the sinking.

Under the combined fire of Jellicoe's dreadnoughts and Beatty's battlecruisers, both Hipper's battlecruisers and Scheer's leading dreadnoughts suffered a tremendous bombardment. Unable to devise a fighting response to Jellicoe's deployment embracing him in a semi-circle of firing dreadnoughts, Scheer ordered a 'battle turn away' at 6.35pm, and his ships disappeared with British gunfire ceasing at 6.42pm. At 6.54pm Beatty turned his battlecruisers through a complete circle and lost touch with Hipper, but re-established contact with Jellicoe's van dreadnoughts.

At 6.55pm Scheer reversed his ships back to an easterly course. The only explanation for this move was that Scheer hoped to pass to the north

HMS *Indomitable*, with torpedo nets and booms removed. The gun director and rangefinders are clearly visible. With naval action confined to the North Sea, long-range wireless equipment is no longer necessary and the tall topmasts have been struck. (IWM)

of Jellicoe's rear dreadnoughts, which were last seen by the flashes of their gunfire steaming to the south-east. In a further display of complete tactical unawareness, Scheer steered his fleet directly towards the centre of Jellicoe's line of battle with Hipper's battlecruisers in the lead.

At 7.10pm Hipper's battlecruisers came under fire and by 7.15pm the majority of British dreadnoughts and battlecruisers were pouring a hail of shells on the battlecruisers and Scheer's leading dreadnoughts. The German ships were unable to return fire as they could not sight the Grand Fleet because of the increasingly bad visibility. At 7.13pm Scheer in desperation ordered the battlecruisers to charge the enemy, and the *Derfflinger, Seydlitz, Moltke* and *Von der Tann* sailed on their 'death ride'. Scheer changed this order at 7.14pm and ordered them to engage Jellicoe's van, which they did at 7.17pm. At 7.15pm Scheer ordered his torpedo-boat flotillas to attack and generate a smoke screen to hide the retreat of his dreadnoughts which he ordered at 7.18pm. By 7.22pm Scheer's ships had disappeared into the mist, and the torpedo attack forced Jellicoe to turn his dreadnoughts away to avoid the torpedoes. Scheer's fleet suffered 27 hits, of which 19 hit battlecruisers. In the *Derfflinger* both aft gun turrets were hit and pierced, with cordite fires burning out both turrets, but the ship did not explode and sink.

Beatty re-sighted the German battlecruisers at 7.47pm and closed to engage. The light was disappearing as the sun set. At 8.19pm, *Princess Royal* opened fire at 12,000 yards (11,000m) on *Seydlitz*, scoring two hits. *New Zealand* opened fire at 8.21pm and hit *Seydlitz* three times at 9,000 yards (8,200m). *Lion* opened fire at 8.23pm and obtained one hit on *Derfflinger*. By 8.30pm the German battlecruisers had turned away again and were lost in the darkness. The final shooting by British battlecruisers was between 8.30pm and 8.40pm when *Princess Royal, Tiger, New Zealand* and *Indomitable* fired at German pre-dreadnoughts, registering three hits. At 8.40pm with the ceasefire gongs ringing, the battle of Jutland ended for the British battlecruisers.

During the night Scheer escaped across the stern of the Grand Fleet and reached the safety of the German minefields. For the British, the battle was an unpalatable disappointment. Britain remained in command of the seas, but the loss of three battlecruisers, three armoured cruisers, two of them also by magazine explosions, and eight destroyers was a bitter pill for the public. German losses were one battlecruiser, one pre-dreadnought battleship, four light cruisers and five torpedo boats. After the battle the key question was: Why did three battlecruisers explode?

Beatty telegraphed Jellicoe on 3 June as follows:

'Urgent

Experience of *Lion* indicates that open magazine doors in turrets are very dangerous. Present safety arrangements of flash doors in are ineffective when turret armour is penetrated. Flash from shell may reach cordite in main cages and thence to handling rooms. This occurred in *Lion* when turret roof was penetrated, but magazine doors being at once closed saved magazine from catching fire. Almost certain that magazines of three lost battlecruisers exploded from such cause. Consider matter of urgent necessity to alter existing communication between magazine and handling rooms by reverting to original system of handling room supply scuttles, which should be fitted immediately. Meanwhile consider imperative to maintain small stock cordite in handling room for magazine, doors being kept closed with one clip on and opened only for replacement of handling room. Proposed handling room supply scuttles should be capable of being made watertight at will. Commander Dannreuther of *Invincible* will report personally on this matter at Admiralty to-morrow Sunday.'

Beatty's recommendation echoed the changes Warrant Officer Grant had made on board *Lion* in 1915, but had not been made in the other ships of the Battlecruiser Fleet. The First Lord of the Admiralty advised his fellow cabinet members on 5 June that the reason the three battlecruisers sank was because of unsafe cordite management.

It was unpalatable to the officers of the Battlecruiser Fleet and Grand Fleet that the reason three battlecruisers exploded was because of unsafe cordite-handling procedures; in effect, they were responsible for sinking themselves. Jellicoe advised the First Sea Lord that the heavy losses were because of 'inadequate protection' and this gave rise to the now widely held view that British battlecruisers were under-armoured. A detailed review by the Third Sea Lord, Rear Admiral Tudor, who interviewed the few survivors from the sunken battlecruisers including Commander Dannreuther the gunnery officer of *Invincible*, concluded that gun crews in their effort to speed up the supply of cordite to the guns had stacked large numbers of unprotected cordite charges outside the magazine in the handling room, the working chamber and the turret itself as 'ready-use'. Tudor's report was circulated in November 1916. On 22 November 1916, Jellicoe was appointed First Sea Lord, with Beatty taking over as Commander-in-Chief of the Grand Fleet. In the new Admiralty regime, Tudor was sent to command the China Station, and his report was filed. All battlecruisers were refitted with additional armour, improved flash-tight turret fittings were installed, and the Battlecruiser Fleet mandated that minimal cordite charges be stacked in the magazine handling room.

The raid on Tondern

On 17 July 1918, *Furious* left Rosyth, together with the 1st Light Cruiser Squadron, carrying seven Sopwith 2F.1 Camel aircraft, each equipped with two 50lb (23kg) bombs. *Furious* closed the Danish coast near the Linkoeping Lighthouse, and at 3am launched its aircraft. The aircraft followed the coast southwards until they passed over the German border, where they turned east and followed the road to Tondern. At 4.35am the aircraft bombed the giant Toska hangar, and two Zeppelins, *L54* and *L60*, were destroyed. The Tobias hangar, containing a captive balloon, was also set on fire and destroyed.

This raid by *Furious*, carried out at a range of approximately 100 miles (160km), was the first successful carrier strike in history and marked the end of the series of actions undertaken by battlecruisers during 1914–1918.

The surrender of the High Seas Fleet

On 21 November 1918, the High Seas Fleet surrendered and the battlecruisers *Hindenburg, Derfflinger, Seydlitz, Moltke* and *Von der Tann* passed into captivity at the Firth of Forth. The next day they were escorted by the 1st Battlecruiser Squadron to Scapa Flow, the furthest that German battlecruisers had ever sailed from port during the war. The German battlecruisers ignominiously scuttled themselves on 21 June 1919.

CONCLUSION

British battlecruisers were designed to enforce Britain's command of the sea globally, and played a dominant role in dictating that the battle space for the naval war was the North Sea. Whilst British battlecruisers imposed their will on the enemy to retain command of the sea, they suffered from a series of operational problems that collectively gave rise to their reputation of being a 'flawed design'.

Battlecruisers, with the exception of *Queen Mary*, were fitted with the inadequate Dreyer fire-control system that could not cope with the ranges and changes in the range to enemy ships that battlecruisers fought at. This was compounded by rangefinders that were not accurate for gunfire above a range of 10,000 yards (9,150m). Gunnery practice is critical for gunnery accuracy. Battlecruisers based at Rosyth had no protected area where they could undertake gunnery practice. In the six months prior to Jutland, the battlecruisers were only able to undertake one battle target practice. The Grand Fleet could conduct gunnery practice within Scapa Flow. The High Seas Fleet could practice in Kiel Bay and the Baltic. The armour-piercing shells supplied to the Royal Navy were known to be inadequate in 1910. The lack of effective offensive weapons compromised the ability to damage the enemy and prevent them from inflicting damage in reply.

The Battlecruiser Fleet attempted to overcome the lack of gunnery practice and inadequate fire-control equipment by concentrating on 'rapid fire' after the battle of Dogger Bank. This involved loading and reloading the guns in the shortest time possible. Constantly repeated gun-loading exercises were carried out both at sea and at the battlecruisers' anchorage at Rosyth. Warrant Officer Grant was appointed Chief Gunner on board *Lion* in 1915, and in his unpublished memoirs recounts how gunnery officers and turret crews bypassed established safe ammunition-handling procedures to speed up the supply of ammunition to the guns.

Each shell requires four cordite charges to be fired. Each cordite charge is encased in a silk bag and at one end is a pouch containing 16oz (454g) of gunpowder, which acts as the igniter to explode the cordite when the gun is fired. The igniter pouch is protected by a thick layer of paper which is removed before loading. Two cordite charges are held in a container that is stored in a magazine. Grant found that in action the magazine crews would remove the lids from the cordite containers; charges were removed and stacked in the magazine aisles, and outside the magazine in the handling room. The protective cover over the igniter was removed before the charges were placed in the ammunition hoist, rather than at the gun breech. Grains of gunpowder would seep through the pouch material, leaving a trail on the floor of the magazine and handling room. The magazine door was kept open throughout the action. Cordite charges were also stacked in the working chamber, directly below the gun turret. Cordite for eight rounds of fire amounted to four tons of explosive. The

Seven Sopwith 2F.1 Camels being readied for take off on board HMS *Furious*, July 1918. HMS *Furious* launched the first successful carrier air strike in history against the Zeppelin hangars at Tondern. (IWM)

gun crews effectively turned the entire gun turret and barbette into an extended magazine.

Grant reintroduced established ammunition-handling procedures whereby containers were only opened when needed. The magazine door was only opened when required to pass charges through to the handling room. Only one full charge was allowed in the handling room. Igniter covers were removed in the gun turret. No charges were stacked in the working chamber. Importantly, *Lion* was able to maintain a rapid rate of fire with these changes. Unfortunately, although these changes were approved by the Battlecruiser Fleet gunnery officer, they were not mandated to the rest of the battlecruisers.

German battlecruisers *Seydlitz, Moltke, Hindenburg* and *Derfflinger* surrendering to the Grand Fleet on 21 November 1918. (IWM)

Although it was unknown at the time, British cordite MD, introduced in 1901, became unstable as it aged. This was a result of a high level of nitrocellulose in the cordite. This instability meant it was more liable to explode, rather than burn, when exposed to flash. German cordite RPC/12 contained a stabilizer for the nitrocellulose that prevented uncontrolled explosions, as shown by the *Seydlitz* at Dogger Bank and *Derfflinger* at Jutland. Additionally, half of the German cordite charge was in a brass cartridge when inserted into the gun. The combination of reduced ability to hit and then severely damage enemy ships, coupled with tons of cordite charges with exposed igniters stacked outside open magazines was a disaster waiting to happen, and this disaster occurred on the afternoon of 31 May 1916.

The shipwrecks

The wreck of *Indefatigable* was blown up by salvagers during the 1950s to access the bronze and copper used in her construction. As a result there is a large debris field with little of the ship remaining together. However, the description of her sinking coupled with an examination of the wreck of *Defence*, an armoured cruiser sunk by magazine explosion during the battle, and with the same level of armour protection as *Indefatigable*, provides an indication of what might have happened.

Indefatigable was hit in the stern, turned to starboard, rolled over on her port side and had sunk by the stern as far as amidships, when another salvo hit near A turret, and after an appreciable pause she blew up. The sudden turn and sinking by the stern suggests the bottom of the ship by X turret was blown out and the steering mechanism destroyed. In *Defence*, the hull on both sides of the ship adjacent to X turret magazine below the waterline has been destroyed. This resulted in *Defence* sinking like a stone but remaining upright on the sea bed.

The appreciable pause between shells hitting near *Indefatigable*'s A turret and the explosion is consistent with the exploding shell causing flash to explode the magazine after reaching unprotected cordite. If the shell had reached the magazine and exploded, there would have been no pause – the shell hit and explosion would have been instantaneous.

There is a strong consistency in the reports on the sinking of *Queen Mary*. The first explosion vented from behind the foremast and the ship broke in two. This venting coincides with the ventilation hatches around the fore funnel, below which is the forward boiler room. The boiler room was not the source of the explosion, but the 4-in. magazine which is directly forward of the boiler room and abuts it must have been. This suggests that the shells hit the port shelter deck adjacent to the bridge superstructure, penetrated through to the 4-in. gun secondary battery, exploded and set off the ready-use 4-in. cordite charges, which flashed down the ammunition hoist to the 4-in. magazine. The magazine exploded through the forward boiler room and up the ventilation hatches as this path represented the line of least resistance. However, the explosion from the 4-in. magazine reached the magazine for the 13.5-in. guns which is located between A and B turret and was the cause of the second explosion referred to by Midshipman Owens as he emerged from *Queen Mary*'s X turret.

The wreck of *Queen Mary* covers three distinct areas, as revealed by side-scan sonar. The shattered bow section has a 13.5-in. gun pointing to the surface, with its breech buried in the sea bed. The bow is pointing to starboard relative to *Queen Mary*'s course at the time of her sinking. This is followed by another debris field containing boilers from the forward boiler room. The last section is the midships/stern section, approximately 360ft (110m) long, which drifted over the other two sections before sinking. The hull came to rest inverted. As the ship's hull has deteriorated it has exposed Q turret shell room and magazine, located between boiler and engine rooms. Unexploded shells and cordite cases abound around the hoist mechanism.

Both Q and P turrets of *Invincible* lie away from the upright stern section of the wreck. Both turrets are inverted. Q turret is heavily damaged with the turret walls some distance away. The breech for the port gun is open. P turret is relatively undamaged although one gun is missing. The escape hatch from the silent cabinet, at the rear of the turret, is partially open. X turret remains upright, although the decks around the turret have collapsed. A portion of the armoured plate surrounding the working chamber has fallen away, showing cordite containers stacked in the chamber rather than in the magazine, supporting Grant's description of how gun crews bypassed safe ammunition-handling procedures.

If *Indefatigable*, *Queen Mary* and *Invincible* had followed the ammunition procedures of *Lion* and restricted the amount of ready-use cordite charges outside the magazines, they would in all probability have survived. They would have survived also if their cordite was made the same way as German cordite RPC/12.

All warships that are sunk by enemy action must, by definition, lack sufficient armour protection, be they *Invincible*, *Lützow*, *Bismarck* or *Yamato*. British battlecruisers received 55 hits by heavy shells at Jutland. *Lion* was hit 13 times, *Princess Royal* nine times and *Tiger* 14 times. Not one of the 55 hits by heavy shells penetrated the armour protecting the boiler, engine and steering rooms, which occupied approximately two-thirds of the space within the battlecruisers' hulls.

The bow and stern sections of HMS *Invincible* remain visible, whilst their broken ends rest on the sea bed. HMS *Badger* is approaching to pick up survivors. (IWM)

On the German side, the *Lützow, Derfflinger, Seydlitz* and *Von der Tann* all had gun turrets penetrated by shells. In both *Derfflinger* and *Seydlitz* two turrets were penetrated. The *Lützow, Derfflinger* and *Seydlitz* all experienced cordite fires throughout their turret and barbette structure but the ships did not explode. The lesson of Dogger Bank had been learnt with minimum numbers of cordite charges allowed outside the magazine during battle.

The problem with British battlecruisers at Jutland was that their crews were too eager to come to grips with the enemy. This was no design flaw. It was not inadequate armour protection that let down the battlecruisers and their crews, but inadequate offensive equipment: the Dreyer fire-control system, rangefinders, armour-piercing shells and cordite.

Admiral Fisher's concept of a fast, heavily armed warship with global reach, utilizing electronic communication and intelligence gathering, was far from being 'an ill-thought through strategic concept' and remains relevant today. Fisher's futuristic concept for the global projection of sea power has been more than validated by the development of *Furious* into the nuclear-powered aircraft carrier, carrying overwhelming armaments, that cruises the world's oceans ready for battle.

SELECT BIBLIOGRAPHY

The author found the following sources to be particularly helpful.
Brooks, John, *Dreadnought Gunnery and the Battle of Jutland. The Question of Fire Control,* Routledge (2005)
Burt, R. A., *British Battleships of World War One*, Naval Institute Press (1986)
Campbell, John, *Jutland: An analysis of the fighting*, Conway Maritime Press (1998)
– *Battlecruisers: The design and development of British and German battlecruisers of the First World War era*, Conway Maritime Press (1978)
Gordon, Andrew, *The Rules of the Game: Jutland and British Naval Command*, John Murray (1996)
Lambert, Nicholas A., *Sir John Fisher's Naval Revolution*, University of South Carolina Press (1999)
– 'Admiral Sir John Fisher and the Concept of Flotilla Defence, 1904–1909', *The Journal of Military History*, 59 (October 1995)
– "Our Bloody Ships' or 'Our Bloody System'? Jutland and the loss of the Battle Cruisers, 1916', *The Journal of Military History*, 62 (January 1998)
– 'Strategic Command and Control for Maneuver Warfare: Creation of the Royal Navy's 'War Room' System, 1905–1915', *The Journal of Military History*, 69 (April 2005)
Roberts, John, *Battlecruisers*, Chatham Publishing (1997)
Sumida, Jon Tetsuro, *In defence of Naval Supremacy: Finance, technology, and British naval policy 1889–1914*, Routledge (1993)
– 'A Matter of Timing: The Royal Navy and the tactics of Decisive Battle, 1912–1916', *The Journal of Military History*, 67 (January 2003)

DVDs
McCartney, Innes, *The Shipwrecks of the Battle of Jutland*, www.periscopepublishing.com

COLOUR PLATE COMMENTARY

A: HMS *INDEFATIGABLE*

The profile and deck plan of HMS *Indefatigable*, the slip-of-the-tongue battlecruiser, clearly show the improved arcs of fire for P and Q turrets, achieved by lengthening the deck by 25ft (7.6m). Additionally, A and X turret were moved closer to the bow and stern respectively, which meant that their barbettes and magazines were closer to the sides of the ship.

B: HMS *LION*, 31 MAY 1916

HMS *Lion* is shown at 7.15pm on 31 May 1916, leading the surviving battlecruisers, *Princess Royal*, *Tiger*, *New Zealand*, *Indomitable* and *Inflexible*. The battlecruisers are opening fire on the German battlecruisers who had been ordered on their 'death ride' by Admiral Scheer. HMS *Lion* is only able to fire with three turrets, A, B and X, as Q turret is out of action, still pointing out over *Lion*'s port beam, damaged from the hit during the 'run to the south'.

Dreadnoughts of the Grand Fleet led by HMS *King George V* are in the distance. In the mid ground is the armoured cruiser HMS *Duke of Edinburgh* steaming for the protection of the disengaged side of the battlecruisers.

During this engagement, Beatty's battlecruisers finally have the benefit of the light gauge. The German ships are set against a light sky with the sun low on the horizon, whilst Beatty's ships are against a dark sky with mist and copious amounts of coal smoke from the belching funnels of the two

fleets preventing the German ships from sighting the Grand Fleet. The German ships are caught in a semi-circle of firing battlecruisers and dreadnoughts, which they cannot see, other than their gun flashes, to return fire. They can only retreat once again, behind a smoke screen.

C: HMS *LION*

The first of the 'splendid cats', HMS *Lion*, marked a dramatic increase in size, speed, offensive power and armour protection of battlecruisers. With the blast problems finally solved, super-firing forward turrets were built on the forecastle deck. The placing of Q turret between the second and third funnels constrained the arc of fire of this turret. The objective of this layout of Q and X turrets was to decrease the target area of these two gun turrets, preventing both turrets being knocked out by one hit.

HMS *Lion*, as the lead ship, took the most damage of the surviving battlecruisers during the 1914–18 war. She was hit 17 times at Dogger Bank and 13 times at Jutland, with the hit on Q turret causing the most casualties.

D: HMS *INVINCIBLE*

Admiral Fisher's brainchild, the 'greyhound of the seas', was designed for rapid global deployment to catch and destroy any enemy vessel trying to interdict Britain's seaborne trade. An important consideration in her design was the need for high sustainable speed to catch the turbine-equipped German transatlantic liners. These ships, with their vast coal storage capacity and range of operation, were built with the ability to be armed and serve as auxiliary cruisers in a time of war.

LEFT HMS *Indefatigable* sinking rapidly by the stern on her port beam, with the second funnel about to submerge. Seconds after this photo was taken, *Indefatigable* was hit again forward and then exploded. (IWM)

BELOW HMS *Furious* showing her final configuration as an aircraft carrier, with the bridge and funnels removed from the flight deck. (IWM)

A stern view of HMS _Indefatigable_ taken just before the battle of Jutland. The new gun director is visible beneath the spotting top on the foremast. The topmasts have been struck. (IWM)

HMS _Lion_ at Armstrongs being repaired after Jutland. (IWM)

The battlecruisers of both the _Invincible_ and _Indefatigable_ classes were to operate in 'flying squadrons' accompanied by light cruisers, and not a part of the battle fleet line of battle. However, by the end of 1914 there were no further naval operations of this kind. These ships therefore became part of the Battlecruiser Force, whose task was to locate the enemy fleet.

HMS _Invincible_ at Jutland engaged the _Lützow_ and _Derfflinger_, which were Germany's newest battlecruisers. These ships displaced 26,000 tons compared with _Invincible_'s 17,250 tons. In the space of eight minutes _Invincible_ hit _Lützow_ eight times, with four hits being closely grouped below the waterline near the bow. An additional hit on _Lützow_'s forecastle combined with the above four hits was responsible for sinking the _Lützow_. Whilst _Invincible_ was also sunk in this engagement, the sinking of the _Lützow_, together with the sinking of the _Scharnhorst_ and _Gneisenau_ at the battle of the Falklands, makes her the most successful battlecruiser ever built, in terms of battle honours.

E: HMS _TIGER_ AND _FURIOUS_

HMS _Tiger_ was the perfected 'cat'. Faster, larger and with a better turret layout than the _Lion_ class, _Tiger_ was a formidable warship. _Tiger_'s design had been heavily influenced by the Vickers built Japanese battlecruiser _Kongo_, launched in 1912. _Tiger_'s poor gunnery at Dogger Bank was put down to her being rushed into service with a minimal working-up period. A large number of defaulters in her crew did not help _Tiger_'s efficiency.

Like _Lion_, _Tiger_ was able to absorb a lot of punishment. Hit six times at Dogger Bank, and 14 times at Jutland, _Tiger_ remained in the battle line throughout both actions, without any reduction in her steaming ability.

Tiger survived the Washington Treaty, and remained in service until 1932.

HMS _Furious_

As revolutionary as HMS _Invincible_, HMS _Furious_ is shown in this profile as originally completed, as a hybrid battlecruiser/aircraft carrier. HMS _Furious_ marked the formal recognition that weapon-carrying aircraft dramatically increased the lethal range of these ships beyond the horizon and gunfire. The destruction of two Zeppelins and their hangar at Tondern by _Furious_'s bomb-carrying Sopwith Camels, at a range of 100 miles (160km) from the ship, demonstrated this new capability.

HMS _Furious_ survived both wars and was scrapped in 1948.

F: WRECK OF HMS _INVINCIBLE_

This is a diver's view of the stern of HMS _Invincible_, with X gun turret and barbette standing out from the wreck as the decks have collapsed under the weight of the armour. The two 12-in. guns remain pointing out over the starboard side still seeking the enemy. Both gun breeches are closed, ready to fire. The stern sank in an upright position, with the bow section off in the far distance upside down. The teak deck is still visible over the top of the stern hull plates. Between the stern and bow sections is a debris field of collapsed decks, equipment and boilers smashed by the explosion of 50 tons of cordite contained in the adjoining P and Q turrets. The remains of these two gun turrets are some distance from the wreck.

A large curved section of the armour around X turret barbette has collapsed, revealing the enclosed working chamber below the gun turret where cordite and shells were transferred from the ammunition hoist into the individual gun

HMS _Tiger_ in 1918. The midships Q turret carries an enclosed hangar and take-off ramp for a Sopwith aircraft. Training scales on B and X turrets can be seen. (IWM)

cages for loading into the gun. The divers saw cordite containers stored within the working chamber which should have been in the magazine. The seabed around the wreck is littered with 12-in. shells, exploded cordite containers and lumps of coal.

The roof of X turret is missing, presumably blown off by the exploding magazine. The hoist mechanism and cages are missing, but the dividing wall between the guns, holding the wheels for the guides for the cages lies on the turret floor. There is a bird's nest of wires coiled within the turret.

The wreck is deteriorating fast under the weight of the armour, having been exposed to the North Sea for 90 years.

G: MAGAZINE AND AMMUNITION PASSAGEWAYS ON HMS *QUEEN MARY*

What caused the forward section of *Queen Mary* to break away from the ship? The wreck of *Queen Mary* shows the forward section as a large debris field, and there is consistency in the eye-witness accounts, both British and German, that the first explosion occurred around the foremast and first funnel, with the bridge and forecastle section separating from the ship and sinking.

The magazine for both A and B turrets was positioned between the turrets and contained 65 tons of cordite explosive. The ignition of this amount of explosives by a German shell would have caused the complete disintegration of the forward section, and the shock-wave and red-hot fragments from the exploding magazine would also have ignited Q magazine as there were only the large spaces of the boiler rooms between them. This would have resulted in the complete destruction of the ship, whereas the midships/stern section remained afloat for up to 20 minutes after the forward section sank.

Whilst it is impossible to be absolutely sure precisely what happened, the venting of the explosion from the boiler room ventilation hatches, located behind the foremast and around the forward funnel, strongly suggests that it was the forward 4-in. magazine that was the source of the ship's breaking in

two. The German shells probably hit the port shelter deck over the forward port 4-in. gun battery, exploded within the battery, setting off the large quantities of 4-in. cordite charges stacked for ready use, and flashed down the ammunition hoists to the 4-in. magazine. HMS *Kent* had a similar experience with an exploding shell causing flash to go down an ammunition hoist during the battle of the Falklands.

The 4-in. magazine is located next to the forward boiler room, which represents the path of least resistance for the explosion to vent its pressure blast. The exploding 4-in. magazine would then have ignited the main magazine between A and B turrets, causing a massive explosion leading to the large debris field. The broken midships and stern section floated over the demolished bow leaving a trail of debris, including boilers, broken decks and plating, before sinking upturned to the bottom.

A magazine with large quantities of shells and unexploded cordite cases surrounding the hoist mechanism is clearly visible. This magazine is located between boilers and close to an engine compartment, suggesting it is Q turret magazine.

The bridge and superfiring A and B 13.5-in. gun turrets of HMS *Queen Mary*. The three sighting hoods for gun laying at the front of A turret's roof are clearly visible. (IWM)

Aerial view of HMS *Furious* after her 1917 conversion. She is shown preparing to pick up a seaplane off her bow with a launch standing by. Both bow and stern aircraft elevators are down. (IWM)

INDEX

References to illustrations are shown in **bold**.
Plates are shown with page and caption
locators in brackets.